THE SILENCE OF MY SOUL...

MY LAST WILL AND TESTAMENT

KATHRYN MAGILL

iUniverse

THE SILENCE OF MY SOUL…
MY LAST WILL AND TESTAMENT

iUniverse books may be ordered through booksellers or by contacting:

iUniverse
1663 Liberty Drive
Bloomington, IN 47403
www.iuniverse.com
844-349-9409

ISBN: 978-1-6632-3396-7 (sc)
ISBN: 978-1-6632-3397-4 (e)

Library of Congress Control Number: 2021925655

Print information available on the last page.

iUniverse rev. date: 01/06/2022

DEDICATION...

These writings are dedicated to the earth being that I respected most, the one I learned more from than any other, and loved most as "mother", as "family", and as "teacher". She brought me hope and joy and goodness and smiles and laughter and affection and love when I was ten, and I will remember this, and her, always. Her name is Vonnie.

To my TaTa, whose loving arms I cannot forget. I love you always.(September 8, 1895-August 1, 1958)

This writing is to honor all children.

PROLOGUE...

It is probably most certain that my life began and ended (for awhile) in 1958, even though I entered onto this earth in 1952. At age six my life would be defined because of my grandfather's accident. While some of what you will read may seem like that of a lost soul, quite the contrary, it lead to the greatest soulfulness that one could hope for. Finding one's soul, or true (or God) essence, is what we are meant to do. My story reflects that journey and the stumbles made along the way. Some of what I write will cause you to pause and wonder how it relates to you or your life. If you see the relevance you will see yourself, which is always a good thing.

At the age of ten, in 1962, I became aware of the woman who would change my life forever through her kindness, smile, voice, and love, and ultimately her faith. She awakened my soul for awhile, and my child's heart knew she was a being I wanted to love in turn. I somehow knew, at this young age, that hers was an example I wanted to follow because of how she made a child feel. Her influence would be short lived, but not forgotten. Later in life, when I found her again, she taught me how to follow my heart. She taught me how to build my own tree stand so that I would never silence my soul again. Her influence would cause me to write a prescription for my everyday life here.

It will be my greatest failure in this life if, in my final work, you are unable to recognize the reasons for the respect I had for the one that my childlike heart loved as a mother. She answered every question I had, listened to every hurt I expressed, read every message I sent to her, laughed and cried with me, and shared her faith with me. She said the things a mother who loves unconditionally would say because she knew in her heart finding her again was a gift only He, the one she called her "Savior", could give to me. She understood this, and now I know this to be part of my truth, and part of the Truth that sets us all free. As with many books that we read sometimes we want to stop at some point and not finish it. I ask that you continue to read this novel in its entirety, whether you agree with parts, or not. My hope is that this writing will cause you to ask your heart, "Am I living my life in a way that speaks of my truth, and the Truth that I want others to see in me?"

I ask that you reflect upon my story, understand the importance of being in the stillness of your own tree stand, and that of following your heart. Take the time to look inside. Take the time to find the *child* in you, the one that believes in all that is good, and all that is God. It is a worthwhile journey, and a life changing one. *This writing is to honor all children*. This book is about a human journey, and about paying a final tribute to the one I felt most connected to in life. It is meant to encourage you to begin, or finish, your own journey, to never silence your soul, and to write a prescription that enhances your life. Please consider it. The first step is to know how to engage in the act of "dying". If you can do this well your life here will be worth living. Let this writing lead you to your last will and testament.

If within these pages you should find some truth for your life, please contact me at: P.O. Box 375, Millerstown PA 17062. I would enjoy hearing from you. If my words are not for you, please continue on your path, and find the Truth and Love inside of you. Happy beginning, and "unending"!

CHAPTER ONE

EMBRACING ALONENESS ...MY STORY

My preface expressed the opinion that my life was defined by the loss, at age six, of my wonderful grandfather. It was redefined again in 1962, 2003, 2004, 2010, and finally 2017. Why did it take me so long? What part was I denying? What part did I have all wrong? Read and use my example, if you wish. *This will be my last will and testament. I have no more to give.* I have received all that I needed. I've awakened my soul. May your journey from this day forward be your ultimate awakening. Stop pretending, and going through the motions of life, wondering about purpose and direction. If you believe that your purpose exists because of the presence of one person or any person, you have not found your purpose. What is the significance of finding that purpose? Simply put, it is important because it connects you with your true essence, the one that connects you to the One great Connection. If you cannot find your true essence, then you will not ever see it in another being here on earth. Then, you like me, will wander through life as if there is always "something more" you must find. There is no "something more"! There is only kindness and love and smiles and laughter and joy and hope and goodness. There is only you, and the Greater You offering a path for others to follow, by example, not by words or deliberate gestures. Find your soul and let it never be silenced again. Learn from my missteps. Life on earth will never be the same.

My maternal grandfather smoked a pipe filled with cherry tobacco. I loved the smell because I think I would associate it with the times he would hold me. I felt safe and warm, and everything was so right with the world, my little world at age four. To this day when I smell that same smell I am filled with an overwhelming sense of love, or what I perceive to be love, the kind of love that only a child feels and knows. Our times for cuddling would be in the evening on the front porch. I nestled in so well on his lap; I remember wishing it would never end. He had large hands which he would use to pinch my cheeks as a show of affection. My times alone with him were best, just he and I and the stars and moon and sky.

My grandfather was a WWI veteran, and a coal miner. His family came from Tyrol. He had dark curly hair and was short in stature. He was quiet and reserved. I sensed a sadness about him, which probably caused me as a child to want to comfort him as well. He never recovered from his son losing his life in WWII. I needed him and he needed me.

The devastating news for a six year old came on a

Saturday. I remember this so vividly because my younger birth brother and I were watching cartoons on a 1950's black and white television. We never watched television in the morning unless it was Saturday. I have a vague recollection of the phone ringing, and what appeared soon after of the sound of laughing. This did not often happen in our home, so I peeked around the corner of the sliding doors to the living room, to glance into the kitchen. My birth mother was sitting on my father's lap, appearing to be laughing. While this, too, was an unusual sight, a six year old is easily distracted back to her cartoons. It seemed some time until my father came into the living room and told us my grandfather was gone, that he had been hit by a car and died. Everything from that point on until the viewing is lost to me. I don't know if I cried. At age six children believe death is not final, and I am sure I shared that fantasy, or as I now know, that reality.

It seems that the things that are most vivid to us as a child remain so for our entire lives. A child internalizes their experiences, and all senses stay ingrained in our memories. I need only smell those smells or recall those special times to be made whole again. Sometimes, though, the memories are lost to us for a while because they are more than a child can process at the time. It is important that both the heartwarming ones and the less than heartwarming ones awaken in us so that we can know of their impact and influence on how we have chosen to lead our lives.

Repressed memories eventually catch up with us and resurface as mistakes that hurt us and others, not in a deliberate way, but without understanding and insight. We can repeat the mistakes until we accept that we are meant to remember what it was that defined us in such a way, the same remembrance that we realize caused us to lose our way. The two most important memories of my life were lost to me for a time. One evolved around the concept of forgiveness. You see, my grandfather was killed by a drunk driver. He had been walking in his yard some distance from the road when this particular driver swerved into the yard, and struck him. He died instantly. He had been sitting on that same porch we huddled together on so many times, just before he started to take that fateful walk.

The viewing remains my clearest image of that time in August of 1958. In those days many of Catholic faith held the viewing in their homes. Such was the case with my grandfather. He appeared to be sleeping as I looked at him lying in his casket. This of course was my first experience with what we call "death". I wasn't afraid. I remember a lot of conversation, though, about "forgiveness". No retribution was sought against the driver, who strangely had been home on furlough when he committed this tragic error. Whatever these conversations consisted of led me to somehow never feel anger toward a man who changed the life of a six year old forever. But "forgiveness" would resurface again and again in other aspects of my life in a way that caused me to almost become obsessed with understanding this ideal. I finally did understand, and I will talk of this later. But the experience of losing my Tata led me to choose a career which entailed a pursuit of reconciling with the disease of addiction.

I took a vow of sorts at the age of six, the vow to care for those most vulnerable, and to learn the answer to why someone would drink so much that they would drive off the road and kill another, the another being someone I adored. I didn't realize at the time that this vow would ultimately haunt me, consume my life and thwart my spiritual growth. I didn't realize how it would lead to depression, obsession and physical health problems, not to mention flawed human relationships. But I was fortunate to discover the answer to the disease of addiction when, during my career as a counselor, I read an article entitled "Addiction is a brain disease, and it matters". At that moment I knew the truth, and from that day forward I never looked back at the pain of my six year old experience.

I would also be given an opportunity to understand forgiveness and love, at age ten, when I met a woman who exemplified both. But this experience was to be short lived, therefore, I didn't have time to fully understand the depth of these truths through her. It was 1962, and I found in Vonnie the mother I wanted and needed. She entered my life through marriage to a birth brother, and she brought hope and joy and goodness and love and affection and smiles to my existence, and I relished in this as I knew in my heart that she could be the example of change that I did so want. But then the day came when she would have to choose to care for her children, first and foremost. She could not help those who had silenced their souls for a while.

My reaction to losing her was so painful as to suppress her existence in my life, and suppress my memories of her.

This was awakened again, though, late in my life, and it changed all that I was meant to be. She had brought hope to me at the age of ten, and I was to find it again through her at the age of sixty-one. The hope consisted of finding my true self and seeing who I was meant to be. I saw in her who I wanted to be, not as a mirror image, but as one who exemplified that all important Connection I wrote of earlier. She caused me to find it in me, and if you glean nothing more from this writing, know that **this is the greatest gift anyone can give to another.**

Understand, there is an aloneness that we all know, but we do our best to cover it up with our jobs, spouses, children, money, possessions, alcohol. If we avoid it, perhaps it will go away. The aloneness is truly to act as an awakening to help uncover the secrets of the universe, and remind us, of from where we came. The secrets contain the answers that lead us to never know aloneness again. I'm talking here of the kind of aloneness that causes us to feel a deep sadness, a soulful sadness, as if no one cares. But peeling away at the secrets is its own kind of enlightenment. With each new discovery comes a sense of knowing that draws us to the next secret and the next. The secrets were never meant to be elusive or to be kept from us. We came here with them, but we allow everyday life here to push them from our memory. The secrets are the hope and joy and goodness and love and smiles that are meant to be a part of each day. Find these secrets as I did. The process that leads to the discovery of them brings a type of euphoria, the kind that we sometimes fear sharing with a friend or family because we are not sure they are in that connection. Remain in that transition to finding them, finding you, and the most important Connection you could hope for. They are all one and the same.

CHAPTER TWO

THE BEGINNING

It is understood by most that one moment in time can define us, haunt us, and even render us helpless. The same moment can serve as an awakening. Often that moment can happen in childhood when we feel love most deeply and have wishes beyond the realm of earthly possibilities. This is our most vulnerable time because children do believe that no harm can come to them, and that no one would ever really want to hurt them. And it is the time when humans are most connected to God. Children understand, through this connection, that anything is possible and that nothing is impossible. Children also know that death is not final. Loss for them is about not being able to find a toy, when suddenly it appears again. They believe that their grandfather lying in a coffin will rise again, and the thought remains with them always. Only children understand for sure that "going away" isn't the end. The hurt lingers, though, even for the child, as the wish for return never leaves their consciousness.

For those that have a childhood without a significant event, that defining moment can come during combat, from a life threatening illness, from any trauma, from a near death experience or from any deeply felt loss. If we fail to be awakened by the adult experience whatever happens will set into motion a tape that plays and replays in our head every time we have a rocky period in our life. We seldom recognize this "Achilles' heel", the area in our life that can set us off without understanding why. But if we don't figure it out, face it, uncover it, or accept that it exists, our life will be a series of repetitive mistakes. Our most noticeable problem times tend to be repeated in one area of our life. We struggle with relationships, we keep losing jobs, we drink when we know it's hurting us, we obsess over insignificant things, we fail to take care of ourselves, we become ill, we are centered on self through our lack of service to others.

Our hurts become profound, and we look in the direction of external things for our answers, and our hurts remain fixated as they direct our lives. Most adults see life as a series of losses and hurts, and we fail to look for a way to unwrap the gift of pain. It is a gift because it allows us to discover life in a way we may never have believed possible. We don't hurt as a result of an event, or another human being, rather we hurt from our limiting beliefs connected to our goodness, and what we know to be true somewhere in the depth of our consciousness. The pain serves as a way to awaken the truth, the kind of truth that returns us to that place in our heart where only goodness and love can exist. It is a place that children know. It is the place where the connection to the One reigns.

So, unwrapping the ultimate hurt is equivalent to a light suddenly appearing where total darkness existed. We see the path or road again, but this time the stones and branches that blocked the journey are visible as well. Driving over them or tossing them from the path is so easy. We realize they served no purpose, and we laugh aloud for even thinking that they caused us to halt or slow our journey. With time and deliberation we see only the Light that leads where we were meant to go in the first place, and an incredible feeling of calm surrounds us because we realize we have finally reached the beginning of our life here on earth, a place where ultimate happiness is meant to exist. Choosing to find the beginning of a new life, by facing the worst pain, will allow us to face the end of life here, with the knowledge that our existence had purpose. This is often the most pressing question that we want answered as we are about to leave. "Did my life have purpose?" Enter into the place of eternal Oneness, trusting that you fulfilled your purpose, *the purpose* that is the same for all of us.

CHAPTER THREE

THE ACT OF "DYING"

Leaving this existence is no different than coming into this existence. It is through a choice that we make long before either takes place. It is done with the knowledge and expectation of our Creator to find our purpose and our reason for being here. For those that leave this earthly existence before their "life expectancy", we question why. Except in the case of taking one's life, which one should never do, leaving "early" is almost always about those left behind. It is an awakening for us to examine our life, and find our truth. Instead we often search for the reason they are gone, and lose our self in the process. It is in our deepest hurt when we must find our divine self. If we fail in this endeavor then we can be lost, lost to our self, but also lost to **the reflection of Creator, which is our greatest purpose for being.**

We are meant to maintain that divine connection throughout, but at times we allow others to misdirect us, or lead us in a direction that evades our purpose. We get caught up in the definitions given to us through religious doctrine, by family ties, or in friendships which cause us to move away from our purpose. That purpose is the same for all of us. It is simply to find our true essence, our God essence, our divine essence so that all who come into our path know and recognize the same essence in themselves.

This essence is all that is good, all that is true, all that is as your most valued teacher would portray. Just think for a moment of one earth being in your life who served as an example for you, and influenced your life like none other. What was it about that person that made it so? How did they make you feel? Most likely the answer is that you felt no judgment; you knew you could count on them; you knew they loved you unconditionally; you felt safe with them, and when they departed from your life you felt empty, as if nothing would ever be the same again. This person was one who was trying to help you see your true essence. This was their way of helping themselves to see their own divine essence. If we lose this person or their influence, then we think we have lost our self, and can be lost forever.

The good news is that the feeling that they invoked in us can remain or be recovered if we allow it. If you can keep that someone in your heart always, then you can know how you are to lead your life, and plan your death. How do we define death? It is not "the end" as many assume. It is the beginning; an unending, part of the circle of eternal life.

Imagine thinking of death as an "unending", and a process for feeling that true divine connection again in its purest form. No judgment, no fears, no worries, only love and acceptance can prevail in this "death" state. We can find our self and our truth, and no one can interfere.

There are no "bad" persons, only lost persons, lost to the divine connection, the Truth, and the purpose for all of our existence. Think of these beings as ones who have silenced their soul, and forgotten the Promise given to us from many great Teachers.

Embrace death as an unending early enough in life so that you can make a difference in the path others may choose, and in your own path. Be the example of the one who served as an example for you. If you are a true believer in a Divine Being, a Teacher such as Jesus, or some other great Teacher, then you will feel these words resonate in your heart. Live as if eternal life has assumed the process of death. You must choose, as everything is a choice, in life and in death. Listen with your heart for the truth. Choose long before you leave this earthly existence to accept death as a transition, a transition to the greatest of love and joy and happiness. When you do this you will want to serve as an example of good, of hope, of peace and of joy, and you will willingly share this with all that come into your path. You will want to "live life to the fullest", and you will attract the "fullness of life". Make this your last will and testament.

CHAPTER FOUR

---◆---

DOING IT RIGHT

Doing it right means never having to express regrets. One would think "doing it right" means leading a self-sacrificing life, placing the needs of others first. This has nothing to do with how much and how often you serve others. Serving others, when and how you choose, will come as a result of serving yourself first within the connection of your true essence or soul essence. We are programmed to believe that putting the needs of others first is the way to "pleasing God". Quite the contrary. If you are able to shed yourself of this thinking then you will serve others from your heart, not with the expectation of return at some point. Most of us lead our lives in this fashion, if you do for me, I will do for you, not always in a conscious way, of course.

There are those who would like us to serve them first, would like to impose guilt upon us for wanting to find our own peaceful existence without being imposed upon. Assisting others is so that all benefit, including the server.

What if we were to lead our lives with...I am not here to serve you, but to love you without expectation of return in acts or deeds done? I did not come to make your life complete. You are whole, as am I. We have only to express that wholeness through seeing each other and all others as ones who would intend no harm to us, and if harm should be imposed, to recognize it as one of being lost, and having abandoned their purpose of expressing their divine self. Doing it right is about serving as the example of what our greater purpose is meant to be.

Three definitions seem important in order to accept our purpose and to be prepared to complete our purpose here. The first definition is **Creator**. The second is *family*. The third is *self*. This is what I know to be true for me. If it resonates after reading it, incorporate it into your life for all time. If not, start working on these definitions. It will change your life.

To me, **Creator** is the One, the Divine, the Unending, Love, Truth, Goodness, the Ultimate Connection. Finding our true essence, our own divinity, requires finding the Creator energy and Connection. It is neither a difficult path, nor an easy one, but a necessary one. Any thoughts of a Creator must generate an undeniable sense of peace, joy and love. There exists no fear or doubt, only hope and expectation. Expectation of receiving abundance in all things is all there is that consumes one's thoughts. All of life's struggles are viewed as steps toward our connection to Creator, and our divine essence. The deepest hurts, pain, or loss remind us that we have denied that connection, and silenced our soul for awhile. Nothing, or no one, is as important as to remember our divine self, and the One, and the connection we share. We are part of the One. We enter with this connection, and a few are able to remain in this connection when they transition to another time and place, because they know life is indeed eternal, always and forever. There is no ending, only each day's beginning.

Family is perhaps the most difficult concept to define or redefine, in most instances. We are inundated with thoughts from birth about this word. Most of what is expected of us consists of obligation, and the idea that bonds are never to be broken with this group of individuals. Many times this is entirely false thinking. Sometimes we feel out of place with this group, and never recognize the truth. The truth is that many times we are not meant to remain a part of this unit as it causes us to stray from our true essence, and our connection to Creator. We allow the very word to fill us with guilt, especially when our path must lead us elsewhere. Anyone or anything that we allow to take us from who we really are in relation to the One Divine essence will only serve to bring sorrow and hurt and illness, both physical and emotional. Yet we persist in playing the role of the "good" spouse, child, parent, or sibling, only to find ourselves totally lost. We wander through life and feel we have no purpose, forgetting that family is not a singularly defined word. After struggling for years to fit into a unit which was without direction or purpose relative to my journey, I arrived at the following definition.

"The concept of love itself is not defined by certain beings, rather it is defined by a Divine essence, the same essence that is a part of each human being. That essence is understood and felt differently by each being, and by their level of connection to the One True Divine Being. Each biological human extension is intended to encompass Divine love, and form a unit for the purpose of enveloping and enhancing this Love. It is incumbent upon the biological 'mother' and 'father' to fulfill the extension of Divine love purpose. However, Divine love can't be understood without an open heart and mind. Acceptance is meant to be of the purest form, with absolute trust and faith. We enter our existence with a connection to this Love, but allow life, sometimes, to distract us from this connection because of false beliefs, or lack of effort. We can fail in our purpose in the biological birth parenting role, then our connection with the Love that we are meant to nurture our own offspring with is torn, and the offspring are left attempting to mend this divide, or tear, in the fabric of this Love."

"It becomes important for the remaining unit members to not feel obligated to these biological beings, whether they hold the title of 'mother', 'father', 'brother' or 'sister'. It does not require mending of this unit, as the 'tear' is not one where the same fabric can be found to fix it. It is simply to 'let go, and let God', and if forgiveness is sought, to kindly reply, 'God forgives'. It is, though, imperative to purchase new fabric, and begin to sew the pieces together which recreate that ultimate Love connection anew."

"So, then, who are the beings that I would define as family? They are the ones who, with every thought and feeling, cause us to understand the depth of Love that has no conditions, and is felt from one's heart. If you are fortunate to have as these beings ones that you call 'mother' or 'father' or 'sister' or 'brother', then you are indeed one of the fortunate. If not, allow other beings to come into your life because they are as God intended, and it is okay to call them family. This new family is truly a gift that we can freely accept, and later give to others in need of such a gift." (Family, Magill)

I knew that I had to redefine family, not from a place of bitterness, anger or resentment, but from a true understanding of God's intention of this often misunderstood word.

This is what I believe. Find the truth in your heart that defines family for you.

On *self*, be assured this word never represents selfish or self-absorbed thoughts and actions. I, myself, is only ever a part of the larger Self, the one whole representation of all. So, in essence, we are everything and we are nothing. When we take our emphasis off of the selfish self the only thing that exists is the larger Self. This truly keeps our focus upon the greater good, not undermining or understating the importance of being true to ourselves, first and foremost.

The only way to offer love to another is to offer it through love of self first, otherwise it will become a resentful love, a self sacrificing love, a misguided love, a mistaken love, an abusive love. Dismiss the idea that "two become one" where love is concerned. The Love that great teachers like Jesus, and others like Him exemplified, was to show the love that is innately part of all of us. It exists whether we want to accept it or not. Most of our struggles in life have to do with simply not accepting the ultimate Love in whatever name you choose to call it. We often get caught up in arguing over the name of this Love, instead of just recognizing that its origin existed through many teachers and scholars and theologians, all of whom attempted in one way or another to show us the Love. It was the ego driven man that distorted their words and teachings to distract us from the Truth. The Truth, by the way, is not found in a structure, one that might be labeled sanctuary, or church, or temple. It is only ever found in the heart of you, and in the heart of me, pure and simple. Once you find it, there is never a need to speak it, flaunt it, preach it, but only to live it. Others can then find their truth as they observe this exemplification. I had such an example in my life on earth for a short time. I saw in her something that showed me the life I wanted to live. I made the mistake of asking her to define it. She resisted, as would any good teacher, to try to put the Love into words. She knew I had to find it inside my being, not hers. I will never forget some of her words, though, spoken not for my benefit, but just words in conversation and for some direction at times. It is my hope that her words will bring truth into your life, as it did mine.

CHAPTER FIVE

SHE SAID...

These words impacted my heart. Let your heart decide if you find them to reflect the truth you want for your life. She said, "Childlike love is irreplaceable, pure and real." Other "teachers" have used similar words. Reflect upon this in the stillness.

She said, "Guide me in the way You would have me go." She said these words each morning upon rising, knowing that the "You" was her strength and comfort. What happens when you say these words?

She said, "I want you to find peace and comfort in each day." What is it that brings you peace? It is a mistake to think it is of external making. Can you find peace and comfort in the stillness of a sunset, the observation of a kind gesture, a baby's sleeping essence, the sound of the ocean with a calming breeze? Where do you find peace and comfort? Be in that "place" often, no matter what your situation.

She said, "You will always be part of my family." She

redefined family for me, taking away my hurt and sadness, some of which caused hurt to her as well. She never said that to me; I have said that many times to myself, and I failed her in being the family that she exemplified for me, only to her, mostly because of that belief that I was not worthy of her as my family. She didn't talk of forgiveness but she exemplified it in a way I didn't want to accept or to understand. I knew of her connection to the One, referencing Him as her "Lord and Savior", through how she responded to life on earth, and her own trials. I came to want to share her kind of family love with other beings, so they would feel it, if they would need it, as did I. Revisit your definition of family if you need to, as this can keep you stuck in the unworthiness trap if you do not.

She said, "I am always here for you." This is the most profound of her gifts to me because it reflects the ultimate in Love. There is nothing so true as words that come from the heart of the One whose love is unending. I saw in her heart the heart of this Oneness. These particular words showed me the understanding of eternal life, the acceptance of another great Teacher who demonstrated this knowledge to us in His everyday journey on this earth. Some have understood it from a book they have read. I know it in my heart from a woman I knew and loved. She represented my new family. She walked as part of the Light. It could be said that this reflects a woman who is perfect, infallible, without flaws. Not at all. What it is meant to reflect is a woman who knew upon saying words from a place of darkness, or acting in a way which was more human than divine, how to return with the same effort, to that place of Light. There are others like her who exist among us. How fortunate we are if we can have that one example to guide our path until our path is one which brings us to that place of peace.

Alone with her own thoughts, and with the thoughts of those who loved her as a child loves, allowed this particular woman to be in the Truth. There are words that are said at a marriage ceremony which would best be said in all relationship bonds, "what God has brought together let no man put asunder". When we have found that relationship that only speaks of love and truth and goodness, the one who tears apart such a relationship with selfish motives, lack of understanding and acceptance of being in Oneness, is a being who has much yet to learn. It is best that this being learns what they must before engaging again with another human. This is accomplished in the stillness of the day and night, not through any book or teaching or human being, but in the aloneness of our own thoughts, which ultimately connects us to the One Divine Essence.

She said, "My love for you is unending." Only one who knows love and has felt love in its purest form can say such words. There is nothing to add to such a statement, nor is there further definition needed. If you believe this then you have felt that kind of love, and know it exists in every being's heart, if we only allow it. Understand, it is not the words that make this statement so profound and utterly timeless. It is feeling with one's heart the very truth of the words. If you question or doubt, then the doubt is of your doing, and the work is yours to do. The most recent Divine Teacher, the one called Jesus, said similar words, which few accept or believe in their heart. The heart is key here, as nothing takes place outside the workings of the heart. If this resonates with you, then "follow your heart". She said that, too, to me, numerous times. Three words which carry such meaning.

She said, "I just want you to be happy". These were not just hollow words that we sometimes say to one another. It came from her heart because I felt it in my child's heart that loved her so. Can we say this to others without defining it for them, and just trusting that their happiness will create happiness in others?

She said the words that a mother would say to a child, "I'm proud of you." "You are wonderful." These words made me want to be the best person that I could be, and to live my life as I saw her live hers, with compassion for others and through His love, that of her divine Teacher.

She said, "You show respect by your actions." I wanted her to know I respected her, and her teachings, but not just through my words, but through how I treated her and others.

The beautiful soul who said all of these words departed from this earthly existence on March 23, 2021. Her words, her image, her voice, her essence, all remain etched in my memory. She existed as the "mother", "teacher", and "family" that gave me all that I could ever want to understand the connection to the One. Only children, and those who loved her with that childlike love, knew of her depth of connection. She and her Love are truly unending.

CHAPTER SIX

WHAT IS FORGIVENESS?

Sometimes we get down right angry when someone suggests we are to forgive another. Let me try to help put this idea to rest so that you can define the word in a way that brings peace, not more anguish.

I mentioned that I first heard the "forgiveness" word after the death of my grandfather. I was too young to process this concept so it caused me to choose a career that would prevent any more persons who drank from taking a human life. I chose a career that was meant to protect children so they would not hurt as I had been hurt. But each child I helped triggered in me the old hurt of the loss of someone whose love was so incredibly real and wonderful to a child. So I suffered along with child after child, until the day I picked up an article, the one about addiction, and read what would bring me to a place of peace. An almost indescribable feeling of release overcame me, and I thought that this was the end of the hurt. I didn't realize that I had more work to do, and had to ultimately reconcile with this forgiveness idea.

With all things in our lives that we push aside, deny, pretend away, they will eventually resurface. Usually the resurfacing is much more pronounced the second, and third and fourth time, until we finally have to choose to face this hurt or block or denial, or whatever name you might call it. I finally realized what I had to face was not my hurt, but my ability to find myself again, to find my connection to the being inside of me that felt so wonderful when all I felt was love, in my case, my grandfather's love. He epitomized the love that was the best of love, the love that comes through a child's heart and how a child sees God, or the One or Source, or whatever name you give it. A child enters with this knowing, and recognizes it in others easily, and wants it over and over. My grandfather felt it, too, from me, and so our relationship generated such a bond that it never left my memory.

Once I understood the disease of addiction and alcoholism I was able to find peace with this time in my life but I didn't continue my work here because I failed to realize that I had not made peace with the forgiveness factor, so to speak. Why is this important? If we fail, as I did, to understand the meaning of forgiveness, then we cannot feel that connection that makes us complete and one with our soul self, and our divine essence. This is the God in us. This is the being inside of us that was exemplified by numerous great Teachers, among them being Jesus. Sadly, though we have taken the words of beings like Jesus out of context when it comes to some of the most necessary ways to find that divinity in ourselves. The biggest fallacy related to forgiveness is the one surrounding these words, "Father, forgive them, they know not what they do." Think on this for a time; "think" with your heart. I will tell you later of what my heart revealed to me.

CHAPTER SEVEN

THE PURPOSE OF "TRIALS"

It was 2003, and my doctor was on the phone with me at 8AM. Doctors seldom call directly, and certainly not at that hour, with good news. His first words were, "There is no cancer of the brain." This statement was made with regard to the findings on my recent brain MRI. "But you do have a rare congenital brain disorder called Chiari I Malformation with syringomyelia". He had no experience with this disorder, nor did I. I guess my mind must have drifted off at hearing this because I can't recall the rest of the conversation. I had been experiencing symptoms for almost eleven years, and had been misdiagnosed with having diabetes, depression, a thyroid problem, iron deficiency, strep throat, possible seizure disorder, some eye problem, possibly brain cancer, possibly MS. I could sense that both family doctors who had been treating me all these years felt badly. But the MRI was quite clear in showing what was happening to me medically. It was suggested I see a neurologist as soon as possible. I had a different plan in mind.

Soon after the call I started to research the disorder, and discovered there was no cure for it. It is an unusual disorder in that one can look quite normal to the outside world while experiencing a multitude of symptoms, most of which exist inside the brain. For those eleven years I had been fatigued, had balance issues when walking, had visual distortions, had numbness of extremities, had hearing distortions, swallowing problems, had anxiety, and probably was depressed because of all of this. I kept my health concerns to myself for two reasons, the most important one being that my eldest birth sister was going through cancer treatment, and I wanted to be there for her, and the other reason being that I wasn't sure of my prognosis.

I had been diligently searching for a cure for my sister who had nonsmall cell lung cancer. I began a search for clinical trials for my disorder. I was so torn up about this that I began to question why this happened now. It seemed that I must make a choice between helping my sister and helping myself. What kind of choice was that to make? I began to regress spiritually wondering if this was meant to be some kind of test. I knew that I wanted my sister to live more than I wanted to live, yet something told me that was not part of the choice in the why of this. This seemed to put me at a crossroads again to search for that Truth that exists in all of us.

I had hoped most of my career I had offered healing in some capacity or another to children, parents, addicts, those diagnosed with mental health issues, veterans, the incarcerated. But was I a healer as I viewed the great Healer, even if in a much less significant way? I found out that my healing was only superficial, not the kind of healing that made my sister's cancer go away, or gave the healing needed for the one who served as mother and teacher to me. Twice I wanted to give my life for the two persons who loved me unconditionally, and twice it was not to happen. What Truth was I not understanding, and what work had I not yet done in my life?

I found a clinical trial going on at NIH, the National Institutes of Health, for my disorder. As soon as the neurosurgeon saw my MRI he wanted to immediately schedule decompression brain surgery. He told me that the risk of choking to death was imminent. I was finishing up a children's program I had created, and I wanted to see it through, so I scheduled the surgery a month later. I was glad to participate in a study hoping that it would serve to help others and help to find a cure for this disorder. Having no children of my own, I felt this would be my only legacy.

The process of completing a living will, and the one read after death, is a soul searching one. I believed I would not survive the surgery, or hoped I would not, so that my lungs could be harvested for my sister. I left a directive saying so, and instructed the neurosurgeon to see to it that it would happen. Facing the end of one's life awakens all channels, and the truth of one's existence and one's actions throughout a lifetime surface in bold print. I did not fully process this until my sister passed, but I knew I had not lived my life in a way that carried any heavy baggage, the kind that called for restitution. I had attended enough AA meetings to know what this entailed. I tried to do right by others, help others, and I knew I had not done anything to deliberately hurt another.

It is true, though, that a life threatening illness or pending death removes any desire to deceive. Undeniable honesty prevails at this time. The light appears again, or for the first time for some, and we should all pray at these times that it never dims or goes out, because to see the Light, and then deny it, is to commit the "unforgivable sin". If only we would live each day remembering that Light, and how we are here to help shine it upon others, and to allow it to shine in us so that others may see it. Regardless, we must learn to finish each day without regret, and to resolve any part we may have had in a wrongdoing before the end of the day. More importantly, it is *not* for us to resolve the transgressions of another. It is for each being to take that upon themselves. Some may choose not to do so, and that is their free will. These we must give to a greater Light. This particular trial gave me pause to find that Light in me again, and I was grateful for the reminder.

I could not save my sister by giving her my lungs as I survived my surgery, and was left to continue on this earthly journey. I can tell you with assurance that survivor's guilt is real, and one I would not wish upon any other being. But what she left for me as a legacy is a gift for all time, and one I try to use each day to show my gratitude. I'll share this gift later with you, and how Vonnie made it real again.

CHAPTER EIGHT

MY EARTH SISTER

This woman, too, knew of her Creator's love, and exhibited it in her life over and over again. She, like the woman I respected most, gave comfort to others, and offered the most answered prayers. Whenever I was hurt or hospitalized she would appear, and I knew I would be okay. She had a great earth teacher in her life, too, her grandmother, and her namesake. Her grandmother would be her spiritual mentor and bring healing to her at age 20 when an elusive illness overcame her.

Sue was ill for months without doctors being able to find a diagnosis. Our grandmother took her to Florida for a year, and she returned well. Her words would reflect that time, *"Grandma Anna Susan took me to Florida, and 'healing' took place. How much of that healing related to her quiet prayers and meditation I will never know, but I did know the power of her prayers."*

"From the first moment I became aware of her being, I sensed that she had a special prescription for me. She was able to enhance

my desire to read, to discover, to appreciate, to dream and to discriminate the worthwhile from the trivial. As my Bible School teacher she transformed the 'assignment' of memorizing the 23rd Psalm into a guidepost for living. Her method of teaching moral and spiritual values was an amalgamation of loving precepts and examples. She was able to fill the voids that parents might inadvertently overlook, and gave appropriate therapy to my concerns, secret fears, and my dreams."

Sue attended her grandmother's alma mater, and wanted so much for her to see her graduate. She would speak of it in this way, *"Grandma and I talked at length about the joy of my graduation, but God, in his inscrutable wisdom, took this noble soul unto himself. I felt her presence that day and her spiritual presence has always remained with me-the physical void was and has been something else."*

Sue was to be diagnosed with cancer in her early 50s, and transitioned from this earthly existence on February 7, 2004. She was 55 years young. It is a day I cannot forget. Here are the events of that day, as I wrote them a year after her transition. "The aloneness of sitting there at four in the morning, occasionally glancing at her lying so still, positioned so carefully by the nurse, is my most surreal memory. Everyone had said their goodbyes, but I kept watch over her for about a half hour before they came to pick her up. I had to protect her, to keep her safe. I wanted, no needed, to be sure she would be handled carefully. The nurse promised me that they would not use a body bag or cover her face. But they did bring a body bag, and when they saw me sitting there still, they left her face uncovered. I walked out with her that morning; it was cold and wet.

As we approached the door of the Hospice facility, the driver stopped for a moment. I touched my sister's cheek with the back of my hand, and as I did I knew in my heart that her life had not ended, but just begun. She seemed more alive at this moment than ever before. What did this mean? Why had she passed from her earthly existence on my birthday?"

"My thoughts drifted to attempting to understand what this final day meant. I knew if I didn't face this ultimate hurt, I would not recover, and be lost forever. I have only to breathe right now. If I can breathe then I can learn. I was one of those beings who spent time focused on how I should find answers for others, never myself. What questions should I ask? What answers do I need? My sister believed in 'eternal life', and I knew her previous attempts to help me understand these two words of Truth, were about to change my world."

"I got into my car to drive the three or so hours to my home. As is not unusual for me, I soon found myself lost, in downtown Washington DC, no less. It was desolate at 5AM and the only humans apparent to me were ones I was fearful to ask at that hour. I pulled the car to the side of the road, and with a frightened voice said, 'Sue, I know you are not settled in yet, but I need your help.'. In an instance, a black man walked out of a building near my car. With complete calm, I got out of my car and said to the man, 'I am lost'. That statement was true in so many ways, but he understood its immediate intent and told me to follow him in his car. My heart told me my sister had sent him for two reasons. One, she had spoken many times of how she had been so spiritually uplifted by a black community church service she had attended. Two, she had always been there when I needed her most, and I knew in my heart she would not abandon me. I followed this man until the interstate appeared and I could proceed on my way home."

"I will never know for sure if this man existed in reality or not, I just know he was sent by my sister."

"Even though my sister had never joined the Catholic Church, the priest who would say Mass at her funeral reflected this same feeling. He said, 'Sue is one of God's angels, and you can ask her to intercede on your behalf.' I had been to many funeral masses, but I had never heard a priest say these words before. I was indeed to ask my sister for assistance over the next years to come, and I have felt her presence on just as many occasions. I said these final words to her the night before she left this earth, 'I will always love you, and I will never forget you.'. I believe with all my heart that she heard me."

CHAPTER NINE

IN QUIET MEDITATION

The Divine Light is in all of us. It is our choice to accept it, or not.

My times of quiet meditation began after the loss of my birth sister. I would sit outside at night on a bench on my patio and look to the sky for answers. It was the beginning of my connection to my true essence, and the Divine essence that exists for all of us. These times brought such amazing insights, and although I regressed again after the loss of my grand-nephew, through the support, prayers, and love of Vonnie I began to become whole again, and find that One true divine connection. Let me share with you some of my nightly visions and revelations. Perhaps they will encourage you to spend time alone, and listen and see what is meant for you as well. Perhaps you will question the validity of these. Perhaps you have forgotten your Divine connection. Perhaps you are lost, as was I.

"It appeared one night and captivated me. This star, so brilliant, so serene, so alive and so alone; if only I knew the messages it wishes to deliver! Speak to me."

'Joy brings you near; sorrow causes you to dim. You are not alone. Children, bunnies, flowers, laughter, a touch, a smile, a sunset; all comprise the best.'

"I am at peace in seeing you shine so bright. I want to be one with you to take away all doubts and hurts. I want to know the Truth. I wait and watch, knowing that spectacular things are going to happen. I don't need to verify my thoughts, or convince others of Your presence. The magic is in the believing and believing is trusting, and trusting is knowing. I will watch, listen and learn. Speak to me."

'I am your mother, your sister, your brother, your father. I am the family you have sought. We are the Love that has no conditions. We are here for you and all who choose to see us. We are here to set you free. We are here to bring wholeness, happiness, love and peace. We are here to show you the way. We are never far away, only a voice, a thought, an image away.'

"Somewhere I have heard these words before. Say them again."

'We are truly one. Be not afraid. Peace be with you. I am with you always. The greatest of these is Love. He who believes in Me shall not die.'

"After hearing these words, I understood that there were far too many senseless passages we were instructed to believe, ones that man created from his ego, not from a place of Oneness. I understood that the Truth was given to us by the most recent one whose name was Jesus. But He had many other names, and He existed in many states of being and on many continents, and in many realms. The Truth has been shared many times only to be distorted by the ill intent and ego driven motives of man. I understood that one of the great Truths is, 'ask and it shall be given'. Thank you for shining so bright. The birds are so quiet tonight. They know the importance of stillness. They honor it and You. Tell me more."

'There is everlasting life. All things are possible. I am the Light. Love is patient, love is kind. I will bring you peace.'

"It is great to see you. You have moved, and are even brighter than the last time. Again, I ask, who are you?"

'I am your sister, your grandparents, your angels that protect and guide you. I am the Mother image that you so desire. I am the best of you. Love others recognizing they must choose their own destiny. We are here for them as much as you, if it is their desire to "see" us. You must focus upon your truth, allowing others to do the same. You will have freedom, freedom to be a beacon of light for others, not to serve them, but to brighten their path. Love and laugh and live. Christ is the ideal of peace and joy and compassion and kindness. It is that energy that helps us find our truth, and the Christ within us. You have sought your truth for as long as you are in existence, and it has been met with displeasure by those who seek "outside" truths. They are not "wrong" and you are not "right". Knowing the Truth is all that exists. There is no judgment.'

"I feel sadness yet at times, but not as I had before. I know this journey is mine alone, but with You it has shown me peace that reaches the depth of my soul. Even though I am one, am I not a part of something more?"

'You are a single entity as part of a larger whole. We are all part of the One, the True Essence, the Creator energy. Every being knows this at some level, but allows fear and anguish and

influence to separate their truth from the larger Truth. When we know the truth, it is not for us to counsel, persuade, cajole, or preach the truth. It is best to send it along with the breeze, the butterfly, the bluebird, the bunny, or any form that brings joy. We exist in the earth plane, beyond it, and into the galaxy and beyond.'

"How do I release the worry, fatigue, hurt or sadness?"

'Choose to say, in this moment I choose joy. In this moment I choose peace. In this moment I choose laughter. In this moment I choose goodness. Remember, the past and future serve only for change, or guessing. Live now; have joy now; know that all is well, now. The time of awakening is now. Receive it.'

"When I see you shine so brightly, I am not afraid. I see more; I know more. I feel the letting go of those beings who choose a different way. I allow them their way, knowing that You shine for them just as You do for me. I whisper a prayer that they will see You."

'Yes, we are here for you and for them. The physical is only of a temporary state; it exists for you to find your divine self, and for others to do the same. We are meant to be as the One. Jesus never said, "worship me"; He said, "follow me". This is one of the greatest Truths.'

(Vonnie would say to me one day, after pressing her for the answer to the question, "What is worship?",

"Worship, to me, is my heartfelt commitment to follow Him." When she said these words, I felt the Truth in my heart.)

"Why do 'tests' appear in our daily lives?"

'There are no tests. Each being creates situations which affirm their misguided thoughts. Release this old thinking. Where the

old resides, the new cannot appear. If any around you continue in the old, separate from them. Be with them, but not of them. Say "goodbye" to those that want to remain attached to their physical self. Only spirit self can bring you to that Oneness. If you have lessons to learn, learn them and move on. Humans assume burdens that are not meant for them. "We" are here to carry all burdens, wipe every tear, heal every heart, and bring stillness to every soul. One human being cannot do this for another human being. It is only the Divine Being who brings healing, and you are meant to be as one with this Being."

"What causes illness?"

'Loneliness, despair, hurt, even anger will create illness. Children heal. Remember to include all children in your embrace. Love can transcend geographic barriers, emotional barriers, and blocks generated by biological parents. "Unless you become like children you cannot enter the kingdom of heaven."'

"What is heaven?"

'It is the place in your heart where the Divine resides.'

Maybe it is my childlike belief that allowed me to "hear" the answers to these questions. Regardless, the answers were clear to me as I felt them resonate in my heart. I encourage you, if your life is not as you would want it to be, "listen" with your heart to that still small voice, the one *within* your heart, the one connected to the Most Divine.

CHAPTER TEN

OH, BUT A CHILD'S LOVE

Anyone who has felt the love of a child's pure heart must honor that love, and accept it as the greatest gift one can be given.

I want to talk of a man I met when I was eight years old, one who would become a surrogate father to me. My biological father was very busy trying to financially support five children so he often worked long hours. He was a teacher, coach, tutor, and when he became superintendent of schools where I attended, he also served as weekend custodian, scheduler of bus runs and classes, substitute teacher, financial officer, and keeper of the key. In those days, the 50's and 60's, superintendents were paid less than 20,000 dollars. They performed all of the tasks that are now done by six or seven employees in a school district.

My father cared deeply about his students, and helped a number of them through tough times, and with tutoring help. He was a father image to many, especially the girls, and tried to be a good role model for the boys. He suffered from PTSD, although during WWII it was referred to as shell shock. He kept busy with school related things because it was his way of coping. It was difficult for him, though, to relate to his own children, emotionally. He never discouraged my relationship with my surrogate dad, as he knew he filled a void for me. I respected him for his unselfish desire to allow my relationship with Ray. In fact, I had a chance to show my appreciation to him during the last year of his life when he was placed on Hospice care. I loved doing the simplest tasks for him, tying his shoes, cutting his hair, helping him to pick out his clothing. My greatest joy during this time was to organize a 90th and last birthday party for him which included his family, and all of his grandchildren and great grandchildren. I know he especially enjoyed all of his students that came to express their respect and love for him.

It had been two years after my beloved grandfather passed that I laid eyes on Ray for the first time. The boy's new physical education teacher was handsome, straight, athletic and honorable. He was to remain all of these throughout his lifetime, maybe just not quite as athletic as when I first knew him. He was a Marine, and his word was his bond. He clearly saw men as superior to women, yet we developed an undeniable closeness that remained throughout our lifetimes. We both fondly recalled the incident that brought us to an everlasting relationship.

"The first time I saw Ray he had his foot propped up on the old radiator beneath a huge window which allowed teachers to watch the busses roll in. I was eight years old, but I was struck by his stature; I knew I would try my best to get his attention. He seemed very alone, and I found myself wanting to hug him, which I didn't do, of course. That aloneness I had recognized in my grandfather, and the same feelings I had for him were to resurface with this man."

"One basketball season, Ray was having difficulty with a few players, and some of the parents. Since my father was principal at the school, I overheard some conversations about this, and felt sad. One night, I decided to do something to help. The family bathroom was the only really private place in the house, so I went in there and scripted a note in pencil on a small piece of paper. I remember wanting to say, 'I love you' in the note, but opted for, 'I like you very very very very much'. The contents of the rest of the note are forgotten by me, but when in his 80's, Ray informed me that it had remained one of his most cherished possessions. That strong, handsome, tough Marine had been touched by something a little eight year old girl had written to him."

"I remember how I delivered it to him one night. I waited outside the gym doors, knowing that he would have to take that direction to get to his car. I waited what seemed like a long time, glancing often at his white Mercedes. My heart was beating so fast I could hardly contain myself. Finally he appeared, and I ran up to him and squeezed the note in his hand and hurried off. I scurried home without saying a word; home was literally across the street from the school. I avoided him purposely over the next few days. He finally caught up with me, and said these words, 'I'll treasure it always.' From that day forward we had an unspoken commitment to each other."

I learned early in life, on my grandfather's lap, and through the actions of Vonnie, that words are not necessary for love to be present. I would struggle later in life to find words to express caring, or my need to be cared for. I didn't and still don't like a lot of words; they seem hollow most of the time. But children feel love, and know that it is real, as I felt the unexpressed love of and for this man.

A few months before Ray left this earth plane, I had a phone conversation with him. His wife had told me he had been diagnosed with Alzheimer's, but our conversation could not have been more alert and timely. We talked of the school that brought us together, and for the first time ever, before I hung up the phone, I said, "I love you.". I told him of how he had been the most wonderful surrogate father possible, and expressed my gratitude to him. He penned a note a few days later, saying, "I hope you find a man that chases after you in the way that you deserve."

My heart is sad thinking of him as not being here anymore, but it is equally full from the love we shared.

And for those who fail to see the love that a child understands, I would say to you, revisit your faith journey. A child's love is at the core of divine love. Reflect upon this.

CHAPTER ELEVEN

A MOMENT OF AWAKENING

The day my father's father died I was nine years old. I didn't know at the time that cancer was taking his life, but I could see him fading physically with each visit until he became bedridden. My grandmother took care of him in their home. This same grandmother would come to love Vonnie and her children. Vonnie felt a strong connection to her. She would tell me later it was her acceptance and kindness, and quiet faith that made her feel loved by my grandmother. Vonnie knew somehow they shared a very important understanding, and that understanding was what I would learn and feel from Vonnie, just as my sister had felt it with this same grandmother.

A few days before he left this earthly existence, our "family" gathered around my grandfather's bed, knelt down and said The Lord's Prayer. This particular prayer had such an impact that day; it seemed to resonate in my mind for years to come. Then one day my sister sang it in church. It brought tears to my eyes. Years later, on the last night of her life here, I found myself asking those around me to kneel and say that same prayer. It was a strange request coming from me as I had for some time felt devoid of being prayerful. It would have even been hypocritical of me had I not felt it so strongly in my heart. Why now? I had said this prayer many times growing up in a church setting; what was different now?

I believe it served to connect me with my sister in a way we had not shared before. I believe it led to her showing me the next day that her life had not ended, but had just begun. It made me aware of how I had misunderstood this particular prayer. It seemed it had been used by me to fill my head with thoughts that distracted me from its true meaning. Was it really meant for rote verbalization? Or was it meant as a divine means to connect us to a way of life? I had never said this prayer for understanding. And months later, under the stars, I was to find its meaning for me, and bring me closer to the Love and Light that my sister knew, and Vonnie would later show me.

I hope these words will cause you to search for the truth of its intent, and to live that same intent. I encourage you to not say this prayer again until you know what it means *in your heart.*

The Lord's Prayer...in my heart

OUR FATHER WHO ART IN HEAVEN

LOOK TO THE SKY AND STARS

HALLOWED BE THY NAME

THERE YOU WILL FIND THE DIVINE

THY KINGDOM COME

EXPECT EVERY GOOD

THY WILL BE DONE

KNOW THAT IT IS SO

ON EARTH AS IT IS IN HEAVEN

HERE AS MUCH AS HEREAFTER

GIVE US THIS DAY OUR DAILY BREAD

ALL IS PROVIDED

FORGIVE US OUR TRESPASSES

PARDON OUR IMMORAL ACTS

AS WE FORGIVE THOSE WHO TRESPASS
    AGAINST US

PARDON OTHERS WHO ACT UNETHICALLY

LEAD US NOT INTO TEMPTATION

WE NEED NOT FEAR

BUT DELIVER US FROM EVIL

SURROUND US WITH THE LIGHT

(Protestants continue...)

FOR THINE IS THE KINGDOM

FOR IN YOU ALSO DWELLS THE DIVINE

AND THE POWER AND THE GLORY, FOREVER!

ALWAYS...LET US NOT FORGET!

A M E N

BELIEVE IT

CHAPTER TWELVE

I AM TEN AGAIN

I would see her for the first time in 1962. I remember as a little girl thinking how stylish and pretty and fun and happy she seemed to be. She treated children with a special twinkle in her eye, soft spoken and kind in a way that any child would relish. I loved being around her. I felt safe and secure again, just as I had with my grandfather. It was evident that she should be a mother, and a teacher and someone meant to love children. I was thrilled and honored when she became a part of the family through marriage. Her wedding day was magical to a twelve year old, and I hoped with all my heart that I would grow up to be just like her. She sang at her wedding, and her voice was unlike any I had heard before. Her voice would serve to calm me many times later in life. Her voice I will always want to hear again.

She brought hope and joy and goodness and affection and love and smiles and laughter to a child who felt lost most of the time. I grew up in a home where my birth father suffered from PTSD, and where depression prevailed. I felt certain this particular woman could change the family structure, and essence, to one that reflected her being. She would ultimately have to choose between caring for two beautiful children, or trying to bring a family unit to understand that Love that I saw in her. She made her decision, but would be judged by others for it, and left to answer these critics. *It is difficult to make choices that can impact someone's life, and it is important for all of us to realize how we may impact these decisions.*

I cried many times over the loss of this woman from my life because I knew that no one could replace her, or be as she was in her love for children and her example of that Love that few of us know.

I saw Vonnie through the eyes of a ten year old, and loved her in the same way, and that feeling was never to leave me. For this reason, it could be argued that I didn't see her true essence, but that isn't possible for a child. A child sees and knows the Truth. And when a child feels such unconditional love as she displayed toward that child, and many more, there is no greater Truth. Just as her display of love for children could only be understood by children, so was my love of her through a child's heart not to be understood. What I have come to realize, and hope that you do as well, is that loving someone from that child's pure heart is not meant to be defined. It just is, and no one, I mean, no one, has the right to judge or question it. I defended her, fought for her, tried to atone for things that were not mine to atone for, only to finally accept that it was not necessary to her or me. She "forgave" ; I kept the anger inside me because I didn't know what she would later teach me. I only knew for the longest time that someone I loved dearly, and who made this child feel special, was "taken" from me, in my child's mind, "driven away".

Her beautiful smile would fade over the years, from being misunderstood, and from losing her grandson. Her faith, her essence and her connection to the One would remain. It was most evident to her grandson, and me, because she allowed us to see her heart in a way that many could not, or chose not to see. Her grandson and I shared the same feeling, the kind that felt love for her, as if she were our mother. She understood that, and made us always feel that she would never leave us. That is the essence of a Love that is unending. I saw His love in her, and I knew every child she had ever interacted with, taught or loved, felt this Love through her as well.

I believe a child's love, the purest love, is not to be taken from them as it may be all they have to hold onto at the end of this earthly existence. And having the love of a child is the greatest gift one can be given. Maybe His words say it best...

"Unless you become like children, you will never enter the kingdom of heaven."

CHAPTER THIRTEEN

THROUGH HER EYES

He was my grand-nephew, and I loved him as I loved all my nieces and nephews. I only really knew him, though, through the woman I respected most in life, who happened to be his grandmother. It would serve as her greatest "trial", and ultimately lead to a hurt that would never leave her. I saw that in her eyes every time we were together. I understood the look, as I felt it, too, surrounding my sister. It was 2010, March 27, to be exact.

The sad news came on a Saturday, just as it had with my grandfather and sister. Daniel had just received good news about his cancer, but doctors chose to do one more treatment, "just to be sure". It proved to be too much for his heart, and so at age 19, he was to transition from this earth. His grandmother, the woman who had given so much to me as a child, and later in life, was to once again show her faith in a way that I did not understand at the time. Even at the funeral she carried herself with such grace, and to act otherwise would have been disrespectful to her. She was the one person in the world that I could never be disrespectful of or toward. She had just lost the earth being she would be most connected to, and feel the deepest love for, and she showed the same dignity that day, when she publicly laid him to rest, as she had throughout her lifetime. She understood something I needed to understand because my reaction after this experience was to regress spiritually. It brought back the sad aspects of my sister's passing in 2004, and I felt angry.

Her example was once again to prove to impact my life, culminating in my final journey to the ultimate understanding of Oneness, and my soul essence. All of my memories of this woman, in 1962, when I was ten, began to flood back into my life. I felt the security and safety of her presence, and I loved her once again from that same child's heart. It brought back other memories, too, the kind I needed to process through the "forgiveness" lens. Once again that word would haunt me, taunt me, and render me feeling obsessed with knowing the Truth. I knew the one I cherished as my mother knew the Truth, and I looked to her for that blanket of security I so much needed, the same kind of security I felt when I sat on my grandfather's lap at age four.

It would be a few more years until I fully remembered the early memories of her entry into my life. When they returned, I found myself looking to her for answers, and direction. I knew she could bring back all of the goodness and smiles and joy that I had attributed to her. I saw her vulnerability, and I remembered mine as a child. I seemed to want to be protected by her, and to protect her at the same time. I felt her hurt, as I remembered mine in losing her from my life at a very pivotal age.

I had worked with veterans who had been diagnosed with PTSD, and now I was dealing with it myself. I had repressed my grandfather's death, and repressed the loss of the woman who brought only love to a family in need of understanding Love. Now it was all to return, the memories, painful and powerful, but necessary, to my completeness.

CHAPTER FOURTEEN

THE SILENCE OF MY SOUL

We didn't talk much of how my uncle was killed. The family I grew up in never expressed real emotions. We didn't communicate well, or easily. Each kept their emotions inside, and so it was when tragedies occurred.

My uncle was a confirmed bachelor, a handsome man who loved to dance, have fun with his nieces and nephews, and enjoyed time with women, but always in a respectful way. Perhaps the death of his only brother during the war kept him from wanting to find a life to share with someone.

Forgiveness seemed to be the watchword again. Sister Ruth reminded us of the importance of praying for the young college girl who had struck and killed my uncle when he crossed the road to buy ice cream for a birthday celebration. He had turned 75 and just received a report of no cancer after his most recent surgery.

Unlike my grandfather's death, the driver of the car

was not under the influence of drugs or alcohol. She had not been speeding. We were told the young woman had to be hospitalized from the trauma.

He was an amazing uncle to his five nieces and nephews and to his grand niece and nephew. He adored Vonnie's children, and played with them just as he had with us as children. When he was with us as children, he was with us all the way. He wasn't distracted by other people or things. When he took us swimming or skating or played games with us, his focus was on us. What more could a child ask!

Yet, with this event, I couldn't grasp what was being said about forgiveness. I was 46 years old, and still looking for the Truth. I was tired and worn from the progression of my disorder, which I knew nothing of at this point. I wasn't yet listening to that still small voice in me. I did not yet know what I would come to understand through my sister, and Vonnie. I had not yet sat under the sky at night, and looked for the answers.

So on a cold January day in 1998, my uncle was laid to rest in the grave where his parents lay. Once again, the loss of my grandfather surfaced, and I pushed aside the "forgiveness" thoughts. I silenced my soul, again, for awhile.

CHAPTER FIFTEEN

I FOUND FORGIVENESS

Many of us have been inundated with the idea that we must forgive others their transgressions, that this very concept is a mandate from God. We are made to believe we are all "sinners", and that we cannot possibly be anything but a "sinner". Some are made to believe that a man called Jesus came to take away our sins. This has some truth to it. It is suggested that He said we are to "forgive seventy times seven". So what does this mean in practice in our everyday life?

This is what I found to be true. You can accept it, reject it, or reflect upon it, and find your own truth. More importantly it is for all of us to find the divine Truth, the one from the teacher Jesus, or other great Teachers. Again, I would encourage you to find the Truth in your heart. If you study, keep looking in a book called the Bible, or listen to someone who says they have been ordained, you will not find the answer. When you listen with your heart, what answers do you hear to these questions?

Would the man called Jesus, or any of the great Teachers, want you to spend your life thinking about what a "sinner" you are? Would the great Teachers say, "It's okay to let others hurt you seventy times seven times"? Would a man like Jesus, who professed to be the son of God, and loved children as He did, want you to suffer? Would the son of God want you to judge yourself and others? Would the son of God want you to believe that we cannot attain the same divine standing that He did?

If in seeking these answers you must say, I have to read my Bible again, and see what it says, then you have forgotten His words, "Seek and ye shall find, knock and the door will be opened, ask and it will be answered...". This is a Truth. It is also a Truth that He said, "You will do even greater works than Me". Another great Truth is "judge not, that you would be judged". A man like Jesus came to us to remind us of how to connect to the One. He gave us the tools, and served as an example of who we were meant to be. If we fail to believe that He exemplified the "greatest of these", Love, in its most divine form, then we probably have missed His reason for coming. We use going to a religious institution as a way of excusing ourselves for doing the work we are meant to do for ourselves. We believe that we have to hear someone who is expected to have some great Biblical knowledge to direct us in finding our oneness with God. We play the game of feeling unworthy so that we can continue to live our lives as if we have never heard the Truth from great Teachers, like Jesus.

It is Truth that a man like Jesus came to negate some of

the old thinking such as "an eye for an eye", but we cling to these because then it excuses us to act in a vengeful way toward others. Some "Christians" actually believe that God wants them to act against others through violence. I would say to them, you may be a "Christian" but you are not a follower of Jesus, or Christ. In what way did Jesus ever exemplify vengeance? I would then ask you to define the term Christian, so I can then decide if I want to choose the same direction.

The one thing I am sure of is, if we fail to live our lives as though a child were hearing every word we said, and watching every action we take, then we have not seen the Truth through the Teacher Jesus. I would encourage all of us to think and feel again of what is said of, and about, children. These are the most revealing words. Most people behave in a better way when children are around, simply because we all know the Truth, and we really do know how we are to act and speak to exemplify our divine self. We came from the One, and so we cannot be without a particle of that Oneness throughout our lifetime. We can deny it, choose to ignore it, even allow that Light in us to dim or go out, but it still exists, whether we are conscious of it or not.

Given "the particle of God" that exists in all of us, how did I come to understand the concept of forgiveness? I saw it displayed in the life of one I respected most, and as I grappled with the worst kind of betrayal and hurt that I could endure, I had to finally define forgiveness, or choose to leave this earthly existence by withdrawing completely, or becoming life threateningly ill. I chose to stay for awhile, and understand forgiveness to be a "letting go", a moving on, or "moving forward", as Vonnie would call it. She reminded me that I wouldn't know God's plan for me if I chose to live in the past. I chose her example and accepted that it was not me who should judge others, therefore believing that I needed to forgive them. Forgiveness can only come from Him, Source, God, if you will. Saying "I'm sorry" is always a good thing, if it is sincere, but it is not for seeking forgiveness from another human being. If you feel unworthy then that feeling belongs to you, and your relationship with your own divinity. Confession may be good for the soul, so to speak, but it carries no weight unless we are working to be as one with our Creator. Forgiveness has nothing to do with another; it has only to do with each of us recognizing that we have forgotten our divine connection, resulting in feeling the need to make a change in how we are conducting our lives.

I encourage you to not use forgiveness as an excuse to not find your true essence, as it is the purpose of our existence, that is, to awaken our soul. So keep "letting go" of the past hurts, seventy times seven times, until it is gone from your being. Let those that may want to impose hurt be released from your life. It is okay to move on from their existence. They have to choose for themselves how they will live, but you need not be a part of it, especially if it interferes with your journey in finding your way. Release them in love, and ask for their journey into the Light, the Oneness that is just waiting for us all. Forgiveness is not a good thing; it is a God thing, and we are a part of the One; we are not the One.

CHAPTER SIXTEEN

MY GREATEST FAILURE

Over many years as a counselor, I had advised people to not focus upon what might be defined as failures in their life. Instead I would instruct them to move forward with their life, and find their strengths and use them to live life to the fullest. I do believe in restitution, saying "I'm sorry" with real meaning, and atoning for our transgressions. I believe it is part of the moving forward process. The individuals at AA (Alcoholics Anonymous) talk of this in their twelve step program. Once I understood addiction, I developed an undeniable respect for those attempting and succeeding in staying sober. The part that I came to disagree with in AA was that the "alcoholic" never seemed to forgive him/herself, as one of their famed sayings is, "once an alcoholic, always an alcoholic". I agree with this precept in that this disease is one in which the "alcoholic" is probably best served by never taking a drink again. The part that always concerned me was that their shame and hurt never seemed to leave them.

All who attend AA believe in a "Higher Power", and they let it up to each person to determine how this Being is defined. I respected them even more for this belief, yet it always concerned me that they carried such weight on their shoulders, to the point of self deprecation. Since I was only ever a guest at their meetings it was not my place to suggest an alternative. I knew, though, that their Higher Power did not want them to spend the rest of their life in pain and sorrow.

My time with "alcoholics" was to bring healing regarding my grandfather's death, and to understand the why of the man who caused his death. I will be forever grateful to AA for allowing me into their midst to find these truths. They were all so kind, and I tried to show my gratitude by showing my respect toward them. These individuals were part of my spiritual journey, especially in helping me to recognize that all important Connection that led me to awaken my soul.

I remember how often the woman I respected most would say to me, "You will never know what God has in store for you unless you move forward." She was right, of course, and was incredibly patient with me when I would regress. She especially didn't want me to put her on "a pedestal", reminding me that the things that she was teaching me came through her love of the one she called "my Savior". I listened intently to everything that she said because my child's heart knew she had an understanding that I desperately wanted. It would be the same understanding that my sister spoke of and lived. The difference between the women was my love for them.

Only one would I love through a child's heart, and that made her words all that more important in how they would resonate with me, and reach into *my* heart. Her voice and her manner of speaking enhanced a child's love for and of her. I believe my sister knew that, and helped send Vonnie to me for awhile, to finish the journey that I needed to finish.

It will be my greatest failure in life if in this final work of mine you are unable to see, through my child's eyes and heart, my respect and love for the one I thought of as a mother. She answered every question I had, listened to every hurt I expressed, read every message I sent to her, laughed and cried with me, and shared her faith with me. She said the things a mother who loves unconditionally would say because she knew in her heart finding her again was a gift only He, her referenced Savior, could give to me. She accepted this, and now I know this to be part of my truth, and part of the Truth that sets us all free.

CHAPTER SEVENTEEN

MY BEST TEACHER

As the suppressed memories of Vonnie started to return, I began to relive the wonderful, and painful parts, of her being in my life when I was a child. The painful parts are no longer important. They were not caused by me, or by her. What is important are the wonderful aspects of that time, and the undeniable impression she left upon me. Her knowledge and understanding that I saw at ten awakened in me, and I wanted to revisit it with her. I wanted to go back and find that kind and loving and fun and affectionate being that had been so real to me as a child. I wanted to heal from that time, and she seemed the only one who could provide the answers I needed. I didn't want explanations of why the marriage didn't work. I knew the why as much as I knew neither she nor I had much, if any, control over it. I was angry and saddened at first when I started to remember. I knew how difficult it had to be for her to assume the blame for something that was not her fault. I wanted to atone for the transgressions done, not because of anything she said or did in this regard.

I remember an exchange, just a few years ago, that took place one day when Vonnie and I were returning from lunch. She had stopped to put gasoline in her car. As she was pumping gas, I began to reminisce about my childhood and her part in it. Vonnie finished her task, got into the car, and I blurted out, with incredible seriousness, and a childlike inquiry, "How come I didn't get you in the divorce?" She sat there for a moment. I looked at her and she looked at me, and we burst out laughing. We had other silly moments, which reflected some truth, to which she would always respond, "It's good to hear you laugh."

Vonnie wanted me to laugh, and be happy and to know her love for me, but I wanted more. I wanted to know what that child in me had seen in her that I somehow knew was so important. Her faith was a private matter, she would tell me, but she also said "You can ask me anything." Some of my questions she answered with a book, and some with passages. These were all well and good, but what she knew in her heart, just as my sister knew, was what I wanted to learn.

What was it that caused me to refer to Vonnie as "my best teacher"? One of the things was her sharing with me her ten year old experience at church camp. She had been so overwhelmed with a child named Bonnie, who seemed so "spiritually filled", as she would refer to her. She recognized the Christ, or God essence in her in such a profound way that when an "alter call" was given on the last day of camp, Vonnie found herself walking to the front of the room. Vonnie felt as though this experience was the beginning of her faith journey. Maybe that is the essence of what I saw in Vonnie when I was ten. I know what I saw would lead to life sustaining, and life altering revelations for me.

Vonnie taught me in a way that was understandable, and real. She resisted at times, saying she didn't want to influence my faith journey, that it was personal to each of us. But hers reflected such love and trust, and she expressed it through her actions more than her words. She slowly began to allow me into that place in her heart where her "Lord and Savior" lived. Vonnie was never preachy or pushed anything on me, or told me I was wrong. She did admonish me at times, but not in a way that made me feel bad about me. It made me all the more want to show her respect and gratitude. As with other things in my life, I sometimes forgot to show it instead of just saying it. She would remind me that what she was teaching me was not of her knowledge but of a Greater Knowledge.

One Christmas I purchased a pen for Vonnie that had written on it, "Best Teacher". I found out at some point that she carried it in her purse. She did understand how important her teaching was to me, but had a humility that would not allow her to say it aloud. She showed me love of family, and I failed to return the same understanding to her. It wasn't that I didn't love her enough, or respect her enough, or that I didn't show enough gratitude; it was because I didn't accept her unconditional love for me, the love that she wanted me to know came through her most divine essence, through the One she held in her heart every day. I never had a chance to tell her this, but I will voice it each day to her, and be sure she knows it when I see her again. I never had a chance to say, "I'm sorry" for not feeling worthy of her greatest teaching to me, her love through the one she referenced as "my Lord and Savior".

I had served others and loved children as much as Vonnie throughout my career, but her service and love came from a place of divine love. My service to others felt like an obligation many times, but my love of children came from my divine Truth, of that I am sure. It also came from that hurt child and void inside me, which Vonnie saw and tried to fill. I will always remember her words, "Childlike love is irreplaceable, real and pure".

So, to my best teacher, thank you for the four bunnies that were waiting for me at home in my yard the day I went to visit your grave. Only a mother would understand the importance of such a gift. Thank you, Vonnie, for sending peaceful thoughts to me at night after crying out to you, "why did you leave?" Thank you for allowing me to see the numerous sparrows that seem to land on my patio at night as if to say, "you must show both courage and caution in your life" . When I find myself sad because I miss you, thank you for sending a 1962 song to my CD player, "The Stripper", to make me laugh, picturing you swinging a scarf over your head. I know how you loved to dance! Thank you for loving me in a way that made me feel like your child for awhile. I will always love you, and I will never forget you!

CHAPTER EIGHTEEN

IT WASN'T MY IDEA

During the past two years I had made explicit plans for my departure from this earthly experience. I had already exceeded the lifespan of many with my specific disorder. I had defied "death" four times, so I had no fear of the "going out" process. Here are the accounts of those four events.

The first time I should have left this earth was when I was seventeen. I had been traveling in my car to work at a nearby restaurant. I approached the crest of a hill, and I heard a gunshot. This was not an unknown sound to me as I had grown up in a family of hunters. Suddenly I heard something hitting the side of my car, and because I had my window rolled down, I felt a sensation at my temple. I touched my face and felt blood dripping. I accelerated the car, beyond what the old Ford was used to, and drove to my high school friend's house. When I got in the door, my friend's mother had me lie down. She called her husband, who was a state trooper, and he arrived quickly. He dispatched some troopers to the area where I had been shot, and I was driven to the hospital. Since I was seventeen, I couldn't be admitted without parental consent. I used the hospital phone to call home. My oldest sister answered, and I said, "I've been shot in the head." Obviously that was not the best thing to say because later in life she was to tell me that she nearly passed out after my call. I was told I was in shock, so I guess I had an excuse.

They took me to a "ward" after all the papers were signed. It was a state funded hospital, and the wards housed almost fifty people, each bed lined up one after another and another, in two rows on opposite sides of the room. Apparently a pellet from a shotgun had entered my left temple near my eye because when I awoke from surgery, I had a large bandage over my temple and eye. It looked bad, but I was told there should be no permanent damage. Later I would find myself laughing at this idea of "no permanent damage" when to this day I am not able to drive with my window down. There are still days that I feel the impact near my eye, hear the pellets splattering against the car door, hear the shotgun blast, but "no permanent damage".

Ironically I was used to guns, and even liked them, not for killing animals, but just to shoot. I had been taught how to shoot by my paternal grandfather when I was about five years old. He taught gun safety first, before I was even allowed to pull the trigger. It was something I valued all of my life, and hoped everyone who handled a gun had this kind of training.

My grandfather would place cans on stumps down on the farm. We would all take turns shooting a 22 caliber rifle. For a child I was quite proficient, and was proud of my ability to shoot. I also wanted to make my grandfather proud. He was another grandfather who made me feel special. He was a man whose word was his bond. He owned a sawmill, and would often confirm deals with just a handshake. Interestingly, the restaurant I was headed to the day I was shot was the one he had supplied specially cut lumber, in order for it to be built. The restaurant was called Knotty Pines from the pine wood my grandfather provided. It was the most popular place to eat in the area, and was a place I was proud to work at because of his craft as a lumberman.

My second encounter with near "death" was on another hilltop. I was approaching the crest of a hill, and as I reached the peak, headed straight toward me was a car passing another car. Since it was two lanes, I had nowhere to go. For some reason, I remember feeling calm and at peace, maybe realizing that my life on earth was about to end. I stayed in my lane, for some reason, but the car heading straight toward me went around my car on the passenger side, into a small section of gravel between my lane and the hillside. The other car passed me as on the driver's side, and although I saw a lot of gravel being dispersed, I heard no crash. I continued on my way as did both drivers, I assumed. Someone, or something had saved me that day. After this second incident, it would almost seem I was predestined for some greatness, but if that were so, it hasn't happened yet, at least not the kind that most of us think of as greatness.

The third encounter, of course, was in relation to my

brain surgery. This time, in 2003, I was hoping to leave so that my sister could live. This experience left me feeling guilty and confused. Why not take someone who just seemed to be wandering through life, someone unsure of her purpose? My sister knew the purpose of her life, and she served others through that purpose. I had served others all my life, but I didn't do it knowing that greater Purpose, or the importance of the divine essence in me. I can tell you with absolute assurance that "survivor's guilt" is real. I know my wanting my sister to have my lungs included me not having the strength to watch her suffer. The one in my birth family who loved me unconditionally simply should not die. It would later be even more painful when she left this earth on my birthday. An even greater purpose was becoming evident.

My most recent encounter with near "death" occurred just over a year ago. Ironically I was driving to a doctor's appointment. I hadn't been eating well or staying as hydrated as I needed to do. I remember driving past the post office, just a half mile from my home, and then the next thing I remembered was stumbling out of my car with the horn blowing. I found a porch to sit on, and I recall a woman asking me if she could pray for me. I responded yes. Almost immediately the ambulance arrived, and put me aboard. The EMT I admired most in town stayed with me all the way to the hospital. He is an incredible man with an extremely reassuring manner. I had watched him work over the years, and felt that if anyone could save a human life it would be him. A state trooper showed up; I don't remember if he said anything or not. I called

Vonnie on my cell phone. Just hearing her voice was further reassurance for me. I know she sent prayers to me in that moment because I felt a calm come over me.

They started off quickly, and we met up with a lifeline vehicle. He jumped in the ambulance and we arrived a half hour later at the hospital. A young doctor started looking me over immediately, and running all kinds of tests. He was a kind and caring young man. He wanted me to stay in the hospital overnight to do some further heart tests. But after two hours being given an IV saline solution, I had energy and wanted only to see Vonnie. I knew I would be alright if I saw her, just as I had when my sister had come at such times. Her prayers did see me through. She brought me home that night and gave me some motherly directives, as only she could.

I had many medical tests after this incident, all of which seemed to verify that the accident was stress induced, and that I had suffered from severe dehydration. I went to collect my belongings from my car a few days later. It was totaled, and had been rummaged through, by the state police, I assume. I guess they were looking for drugs. There were none, as I had never done drugs, not even in college when marijuana was easily accessible. I didn't drink alcohol until I was 21 years of age just because it was not lawful. I had respect for the law, even though at times I have disagreed with certain laws. Alcohol was very present in the college dorms when I went. The guys would use the girls' bathrooms to hide kegs for parties on weekends. Maybe it was the remembrance of my grandfather's death that kept me from participating in drinking.

These four incidents have left me wondering what purpose it has served for me to remain here on earth, while the two whose prayers were answered for me, left to go "home". I had every intention of leaving before Vonnie. I was certain I would, and so each time I was with her I made sure, upon leaving, that I said, "I love you". She would respond, "I love you, too."

If it were my choice Vonnie would be here, not me. This is not to say that I don't believe for one minute that she is in the most beautiful place she could be; it's just that it seems that she, too, understood the greater Purpose, and lived it each day to the best of her human essence. But Vonnie was more than her human essence. She, like a few others in my life, carried a knowledge beyond what most know. I saw that in her at ten, and never forgot it. Her grandson felt it too, and shared her beliefs. She readied us both for what is beyond this earthly realm. I know she felt her prayers were not answered because her grandson was not healed. He was healed both physically and spiritually. The hospital was accountable for what happened. There are some aspects of our lives that exist outside of our prayer requests. I feel about her as she did about her grandson. She wanted his life to reflect the image of how she viewed him, which was through her unconditional love lens.

Not everyone can see into the heart of another, for various reasons. One reason is because the other person doesn't allow it. Another is that we may have silenced our soul, and we haven't allowed others into our heart. It is incredible, though, when we see beyond the human essence of another human being. It becomes a reflection of us, and then we strive to be like them, just as Daniel and I did with his grandmother.

Vonnie told me I reminded her of Daniel. Later I would come to understand what she meant. I know I felt valued just for hearing that reflection. She was his staunchest protector, and I understood why because I saw in her the same vulnerability that she saw in Daniel. Very few knew that vulnerability because Vonnie had to be strong and resilient early in life. She hid those vulnerable aspects of her life so that she could be the best mother and "father" and breadwinner, and maintain that love she so easily gave to children. She loved children for the same reason I loved them. She and I were looking to protect them. Her love, though, came from "His" love, and that's why children felt it so deeply. An exchange between her and one of her students says it best. "Do you believe in God?" one of her students would ask. Her response, "Yes, I do." He further prompted her, "Is that why when we misbehave you tell us you still love us?" to which Vonnie responded, "Yes, God loves you and so do I."

Vonnie gave Daniel and I all that we could ever need. They are together again, and I expect to join them soon.

Vonnie understood the importance in valuing all children, that's why we all felt so special when she was around. I felt the love she had for children so deeply when I was ten that it made me want to transfer that love to all children. However, my need for her motherly presence caused me to miss the many opportunities that children gave me in my work with them. These opportunities were the "pure and real and irreplaceable" Love that is meant for all of us. My focus became on wanting to protect them, instead of seeing what their hurt brought to my awareness. It was so excruciating to watch them hurt because I was seeing them through my adult distorted image of suffering. I selfishly wanted to bring healing to them instead of just loving them, as Vonnie did. She, like other great teachers, knew that healing takes place through the greatest of Love. It doesn't necessarily mean that a child will continue here with us, but it does mean that they will know love in its deepest form. Children truly do know that Divine Love is the only love that we are meant to experience. ***This is the most difficult understanding of our adult earthly existence.***

"Whosoever shall not receive the kingdom of God as a little child, he shall not enter therein, and He took them up in His arms, and put His hands upon them, and blessed them."

CHAPTER NINETEEN

DON'T BE DEFINED...
YOU ALREADY ARE

Many times in our lives we allow others to define us. They view us through a snapshot of who we are, or could be, or have shown ourselves to be. It is only ever a glimpse of our being, though, because they have not seen into our heart. However, once we have seen into someone's heart, it is impossible to forget. We see them as they are in all their divine essence, and we know the truth. But with all earthly relationships, we are quick to forget, allow missteps to change our view, or lose our ability to see them as a reflection of God because we have become lost. Then we begin to define others through our dirty lenses.

What can change our vision? How do we see more clearly? How can we be sure to look beyond what lies only on the surface? It is an age old question, and one in which the answer was provided for us, yet we fail to change our view, to wipe the dirt away.

Each human being knows the truth about themselves.

Typically the one we most fervently deny our frailties to is our self. It's easy to deny them to others. We learn early in life that in order to fit in, survive, or belong, we have to pretend to be as others want us to be. This isn't a deliberate deceit, most times, rather it is the kind that exists in order to be loved or cared for. The most difficult aspect to this human existence is to let go of the need for approval, the fear of judgment, the undeniable need to be loved. It can be a very lonely human existence to find the Truth but to lose those that have expressed their love for you.

So what was meant by the cry from one of the great Teachers, "Forgive them; they know not what they do". My heart tells me it was His final reminder that when we lose ourselves to this earthy experience, and deny our divine connection to the One, we have committed the worst lie, the one that causes the greatest pain. This pain of denial of our divine self is far greater than any suffering that occurs from living on earth. If you believe for a moment that Jesus was referring to the suffering that others caused Him, you know nothing of this great Teacher. He was never about self; He was only about His Father, the One, the True Divine Essence. It was a message that we had lost our way, and that He wanted us to be granted another chance.

And for those who still insist that the "sin" concept is real, consider it as a way to keep you stuck in place so that you never reach Oneness here on earth. It will continue to be your excuse to behave badly, or hurt others. If you believe that Jesus came to "take away your sins", then accept that it is so. Feeling "sinful" is part of the unworthiness trap, and what purpose does that serve you or others? When Jesus was overwhelmed with the "crowds", He went away to be alone to understand His reason for being here. If He is your example of Truth, then follow His example. It is a life changing experience to be alone with your thoughts to connect with the Divine in you. Reflect upon this.

The greatest form of disrespect to His life is not seeing that He was a man who came to be the example of how to find the greatest Love inside of ourselves, and that Connection that we entered this earth with. This is why children are so precious, and were so beloved by a man like Jesus. He knew they understood unconditional love. They carry that with them as they enter this realm. If you believe as I do that we are here to keep that Connection in order to bring others to that place of Oneness, then begin the process of defining yourself anew. This happens, always, from the inside out, not from the outside in. There are no special places or things or persons that define you and me. We were Defined when we entered this world; all we have to do is remember.

CHAPTER TWENTY

NEVER SAY GOODBYE

"Goodbye" to me was always a word that is synonymous with "the end". So I use goodbye only when I want to put an end to something. Goodbyes are for inanimate objects, or to end a hurt, or let go of certain behaviors we cause or that are caused by others. Putting an end to certain behaviors is necessary to moving forward. We cannot see our path if the path is blocked with multiple obstacles, some of which we may have helped lay, and some the result of the construction, or destruction, caused by one or more other beings. Like all faulty construction, repairs and changes can and must be made. These blocks in our path are usually only there to remind us that we have lost our way, and that changes need to occur. Sometimes we can remove the blocks from that old construction, but at other times we need to create new construction, or a completely different road, so to speak. Repairing can be temporary. New construction is of your doing, and may be required for your new purpose.

One day I remember driving home from the town where I grew up. Vonnie and I passed through the place where she was raised, and saw her birth home. She remarked to me, "I don't like driving near here anymore; it is not the home where I grew up." I felt the same way about the small town where I had grown up. It was a wonderful place to live in the 1950's, with especially wonderful memories of the town and the people in it. All kinds of delightful things happened in my childhood there. It was a place where I felt safe because everyone knew everyone else, and so it was like having one great big extended "family", any child's delight. It was good to be a part of a "church family", participating in programs, being in Sunday School, attending Bible School in the summer. One of my favorite songs in Bible School was "Be Careful Little Eyes What You See". I liked the verse where it said, "There's a Father up above, He is looking down with Love, so be careful...". What a wonderful message to live by; it is a simple mandate for how to live, one that even a child can understand.

We are often led to believe that we must leave behind our childlike ways in order to be a productive adult. The exact opposite is true. There is no way to becoming an adult who lives a full life unless it is done through the hope and joy and goodness and truth and love that a child knows. To do otherwise is to deny our divine essence, which will cause us to see only the ill intent of others, instead of who they are meant to be as well.

I could never let go of my childhood memories, partly because they were filled with wonderful moments that made me feel special. These moments existed outside of the home, including walking down to the picnic grounds to fish, spending a Saturday collecting glass bottles to get the two cents, for each bottle, to buy penny candy at the local grocery store, playing ball in the back yard or at the school yard, delivering newspapers to town residents, and being fed delicious cookies as a reward. The children had to entertain themselves, so we left early on a Saturday and stayed out all day, finding lots of things with which to occupy ourselves. And then there was my surrogate father, Ray, and my mother image, Vonnie, both of whom added to the hopes and wishes of a young child. Maybe it was all of this and more that made me want to bring those same dreams to children. I know I delighted in the times I spent with my nieces and nephews when they were little. I wanted for them to feel special, always, and to embrace their dreams.

Devoting my career to children allowed me to remember the child in me, and to try to bring some security to their lives. If I had loved children in the way that Vonnie loved them, through her relationship with her God, I know I wouldn't have become so worn and saddened by some of the situations that I saw each day in the children I counseled. If I had known I had a great partner in this mission, I could have given it over to that Divine Being when I had no more energy or time to give of myself. I assumed burdens that were not meant for just me. I always wanted to make things right for the children I dealt with professionally.

I never "let go and let God" as Vonnie would remind

me later in life. When I interviewed the father who was accused of sexually molesting his child, when I watched a child sketch a bloody drawing because he had witnessed his father stab his mother, when I was told by a teacher that a child was rummaging through the garbage at school only to discover that a mother was keeping food from the child as punishment, when I listened to teachers in a faculty room joke about a 12 year old boy who was threatening to stab a teacher and classmates, only to find out through interviewing him that he had a plan, and was displaying psychotic features, or when I interviewed a 7th grader who didn't know how she had gotten pregnant, I didn't know then how to "let go".

So after twenty some years I became so emotionally exhausted that I turned to teaching in adult education and at the college level. I had to say goodbye to the hurts I had witnessed. I felt so lost in my spiritual journey until I met up with Vonnie again, and I listened to her words, felt her love, and witnessed her faith. She taught me to discern what I needed to let go of, and how to turn it over to my Higher Power, as my AA friends would say. Through my relentless questions to her, she allowed me to see into her daily journey with the One she relied upon through each hurt. Each time I was with her I wanted to hear more. I wanted to know all about those years I had "lost" her from my life. I came to respect her in a way that she never asked for, and she would remind me that any wisdom and knowledge from her came through her Higher Power. Her words and her voice spoke of a woman who knew some of the great secrets in life, but she was humble. I never wanted to disappoint her, so I tried to understand the things that I knew were in her heart, and not necessarily definable. She wanted me to feel it in my heart. She wanted me to say goodbye to the hurts and disappointments in life, and move forward. She wanted me to be happy.

Through her prayers and love and teaching, I did say goodbye to the things that were not meant to hurt me anymore. What I will never say goodbye to is my sister's essence which showed me a new way because of her prayers and love, and to Vonnie, who finished that journey for me. I will never stop loving Vonnie through my child's heart because it was that same child's heart that trusted so completely again.

Maybe the most difficult part of becoming an adult is to hold on to that world of wonderment, of make believe, of play, of trust, of unconditional love as only a child can feel, and know for sure. But, to me, that childlike trust allows us to determine the direction of our life on earth as that of one of fulfillment, or one of pain and sorrow. So, trust in the divine being that is only found inside your heart, and with the kind of trust that comes from a place of complete innocence. We all spend too much time listening to others who have agendas that neither serve them or us. Look for your light, the one that shines inside of you. That Light will cause you to see the Most Divine, and open the gates to the kind of Love that we are all meant to feel.

Most importantly, never say goodbye to that childlike love, the kind that is "irreplaceable, real and pure".

CHAPTER TWENTY-ONE

YOU CAN'T BE "SAVED"!

Now that I have the attention of the majority of Christians who have been preached to, threatened by, made to feel unworthy of, and called the "sinner" name, let's talk of this idea of "being saved". It has to be one of man's greatest distortions and untruths in that we have been made to feel that the concept of salvation is the acceptance that we are miserable beings. I'm sure many have witnessed the adult gyrations, the agonizing, the sacrifices made by those who have gone to the alter. I can also tell you with equal certainty that these displays were followed a week, a month, or a year later, with a reference to themselves as a "sinner". It's not difficult to understand why. The very idea of being labeled a "sinner", coupled with "you must be saved" is the perfect recipe for failure, and for never finding our God essence, or Christ within us.

I encourage you to reflect upon why a minister or priest, a man of God, or any follower of Jesus would want you to continue to feel unworthy, unloved, publicly confess your sins, or have to throw away any fun in life. What "man in his right mind" would choose to be saved believing this! This is the very reason those who made such a gesture in a religious setting find themselves feeling unworthy most of their lives. That's why they go back to being "sinners". I can assure you that feeling unworthy or unloved only ever leads to projecting those same feelings upon others, including our spouse, children or any that may be in our lives. Do you really believe in your heart this is what Jesus, or other great Teachers, would want you to feel, or do?

If you do nothing else until the end of your existence here, take the time to reflect, meditate, hear that still small voice inside of your heart, and "hear" what Jesus said was His reason for walking among us. Don't ask someone else; don't look for it in a church setting; don't look for it in a book; just find a peaceful place where you can hear the answer. I remember a hunter telling me that the place that became his means of hearing God was when he was sitting in a tree stand waiting for the deer to come by. He also said later that when they did come by he just marveled at their gracefulness and stature. Maybe it wouldn't be a bad idea for all of us to build our own tree stand, and spend time alone in it when we start playing the unworthiness game.

It's always your choice to go on believing you are a "sinner", and treating others the same. But don't kid yourself into thinking that going to church once a week, saying a prayer at night, or sacrificing for others is your way to salvation. If you want to struggle in life, feel let down and hurt, feel sorry for yourself, you can do that as well. If you are my age and still looking for answers in a book, a person, or in a church, it isn't going to happen. So before you come to your transition to another life, find the Truth. When you find the Truth, you won't have to tell anyone, or preach it, or persuade others of its realness. If you believe in the man named "Jesus", then please do not dishonor Him by pretending to know why He came to earth as the Son of God. Either you know it in your heart, or you don't.

I didn't get it for the longest time. I played the unworthiness game, and surrounded myself with those who would reinforce it. My sister began my journey into the Truth until she transitioned. She loved me unconditionally, and that was all I needed to keep searching for the Truth. She helped send Vonnie to me who finished this journey for me, through her example, her love and her prayers. I saw Jesus in her, not because she was a perfect being, but because I looked to her through the heart of a child. I remembered what I knew to be true when I was ten, the knowledge that I had been looking for, that had been lost to me. I saw in her the knowledge that this man called Jesus was truly the Son of God. She knew that all we have to do is *accept* the Truth; there is no "being saved". It is a free gift of grace from God.

You don't have to be "saved". You already are. Reflect upon this. I had to, numerous times, until I finally understood.

The day I understood was the day I chose to give Vonnie a ring that belonged to my sister, with a heart attached that read on one side, "love you", and on the other "family". She cried when I presented it to her because she knew in her heart the significance of this. With a heavy heart, the necklace was returned to me. I will wear it, though, to remind me of Vonnie, and my sister, and how much I loved them both, and still do.

CHAPTER TWENTY-TWO

LEARN TO DISCERN

It can be difficult to know where to focus our attention in life. It is easy to be distracted by work, family, friends, or what we perceive as obligations, and to forget the important things. What are those important things? This is where discernment comes in as we decide what really matters within each day. If we set aside the obligations, work, family, friends, what is it that is left for us to do or know or understand? This is where we must concentrate because everything mentioned here is only a small part of the truly significant "work" we are meant to do.

I thought that my work of helping children was all that was supposed to be in my life. I placed it first in everything I did only to discover at some point that I was being drained by it, and doing this work was keeping me from looking inside to find the greater "work" I, and everyone, is created for. It was my way of avoiding that aloneness I referenced earlier.

Children have always made me smile and laugh and

have fun, even though I often would see their hurts as well. Eventually their hurts became more pronounced, and I wasn't able to see the joy and goodness and hope and smiles as readily as I did at the beginning of my career. I thought I had to make things right for them, instead of just loving them through that unconditional lens. My "best teacher" knew how to discern, especially when it came to children. Vonnie would love them unconditionally, which ultimately led to the return in their lives of hope and joy and laughter and love and goodness. That is all that children want because that is all that exists inside of them. Vonnie knew how to bring that out in each child she saw, or worked with, or knew.

Children recognize these traits in others, and when an adult reinforces their world with all of this, they feel safe and secure and loved. That is the essence of discernment, finding the best inside each being, and letting them know that you want them to be happy. It is not for one being to make another happy. It is for all of us to recognize the very truth of each person, and to serve as a reminder of that Truth. I thought I had to make such effort, and do all kinds of work to bring happiness to children, and to let them know they were valued. Vonnie knew that if she just loved them through the Greater love that she held in her heart, that each child would feel this love inside them. I experienced this kind of love as a child from Vonnie. She made no particular effort where children were concerned; she just gathered them around her and enjoyed them as they were in all their innocence. Children don't know how to deceive, and I believe that is why Vonnie and I viewed them as we did.

With children there is no pretense. They are incredible beings with only love inside. It is the Love that is meant for all humans, regardless of age. We get distracted by others, by obligations, by the expectations placed upon us, and we fail to discern the most important part of our reason for being. We fail, as I did, to just see the Love and allow that Love to flow from us.

I was so grateful to Vonnie that I was awakened by her Love toward me as a child. It brought me the kind of feeling that allowed me to be in that Love with each moment of each day. She taught me to discern that nothing matters more than to find that Love in my heart, and just let it be. She taught me that discerning meant not having to try so hard, whether it was in relationships, work, or in everyday life. I finally realized that the best way to show the greatest of these, the ultimate Love, was to just be, or as she would say, "just be you". She saw something in me similar to what my sister saw, and I wanted to just be myself, so I could find Myself, the one that is part of the One.

So, "just be you", the you that knows in your heart that you are meant to be filled with joy and goodness and hope and smiles and laughter and love, all of which becomes visible to any with whom you interact, and who observe you. Take the time to discern and know that all that matters is for each of us to be in the place of Oneness which exists in our heart, and is "irreplaceable, real and pure". At the "end of the day", at the end of this life, all that exists is you and your Creator.

Learn to discern.

CHAPTER TWENTY-THREE

THE LAST TWO YEARS OF THIS LIFE

No one could have imagined the onset of a "pandemic", and the impact, the division, the chaos, the "leaving" this would impose upon our personal human existence, and the world at large. It generated fear, anxiety, loneliness, hurt, separation, anger, frustration, sickness in body and soul, and it generated loss. It imposed upon us the need to search inside to discern our truth, our beliefs, and our direction. Many of us weren't prepared for this. Many of us didn't know how to be alone with our thoughts. Panic set in, and we tried to pretend, shout, become violent, take our own life, all to avoid the important task of realizing our spiritual journey, and remembering why we are here.

Many of us became lost, and realized our "faith" was not as we thought it to be. We were shut-in with some that never really had found God inside themselves, even though they claimed to be "believers". So some left this earthly existence, in mind and body, during this time because of the sadness with which they were surrounded. Some left because of an illness called COVID-19. Some left to avoid having to face that those they loved were not the beings they had thought them to be. Some left through suicide, unable to face the restrictions and requirements placed upon them. Some left because of other illnesses that were brought about by hurt and sorrow and shame. Some survived this time, but, NONE of us will ever be the same.

The only way I could survive this time was to turn to serving others, and to turn inside to know for sure what I believed, and if Vonnie's teachings were real to me. Serving others was secondary because I needed to know if I had been true to myself, and Vonnie, about my faith journey. I could never lie to her about something so essential to my life, and I had to be sure I hadn't. So, as with many of us, I spent a great deal of time alone. I listened to that still small voice inside of me, my awakened soul, the reflection of that Divine Love. I sat in my "tree stand", and despite the surroundings, and what I heard in so many as negative, sad, and disheartening words, I tried to be as Vonnie would be, and quietly encourage others in my actions and words, not in an imposing way, but in the way that Vonnie had shown me as she guided me, never with judgment or suggestions that she had the answers. I knew this was a time that we all needed to face the truth about ourselves, and that it was a personal journey between us and our Higher Power.

I looked around and saw those that pretended for awhile that this pandemic didn't exist, and those that believed that the vaccines would do harm, not good, along with the extreme conspiracy theories on both sides, and I thought to myself, "they really don't understand the reason this arrived on our doorstep".

Darkness always comes in order to see the morning light. It is as complicated and as simple as that, but instead of welcoming the darkness, believing that the Light would follow, many chose to let fear prevail. Make no mistake, those that perpetrated violence during this time, were the most afraid. They wore tactical gear, and carried heavy firearms, and held up the Bible at the same time; if that doesn't say fear, I don't know what does. I don't say that in a malicious way, or even as a judgment. (And it is not a political statement, either. I don't care what your politics may be; I just care that you find peace in your heart.) It just seems to me that if one needs to swing a Bible and a gun in the air at the same time, then probably that someone is trying to make sure they are covering "all their bases", so to speak. Somewhere, though, they know, deep down, the answer is not just in the violence. They were searching, too, but didn't want to be accused of such, in case someone would reference them as a "coward". Strange how carrying a gun, threatening violence, makes us think we are brave. I've witnessed many brave acts in my time, and none were accomplished at the end of a gun barrel. Those that perpetrated fear, in all forms, were lost to this opportunity to see the Light.

It is my belief that an event that is global in its impact occurs because we are being given an opportunity to come together, and to find that same divine essence that exists inside *all* of us. Consider for a moment that a Teacher like Jesus may have come to earth to show us how to coexist in a peaceful way, to find our worthiness, to let go of the "old" ways so that we can live life anew without guilt and shame (by taking away our "sins"), to show us that life is eternal, to remind us of the innocence and wonder of a child so we can find that same child in our heart. If you look at this and gravitate back to the "yes, but" thinking, then explore inside of you what you think His purpose was in relation to your purpose. Come up with your own thinking on the most important aspect of life that you will ever ponder. I'm not asking you to believe as I do, but I'm asking you to stop pretending that you know about a man called Jesus, or any other great Teacher, simply because you have gone to a place of worship all of your life, said the Lord's Prayer, or other prayers, all of your life, gone to the alter as a gesture of "being saved", or prefer to reference all of us as "sinners", and know how unworthy you and others must be. How is any of that synonymous with a man of God? Just asking...and if asking offends you, then look inside to know why it does.

So many different types of "churches" are being built everywhere, and I wonder why. We leave a house of worship because the ordained leader doesn't appeal to us, or the members are not to our liking, or it's not exciting enough. Really! I had to ask myself, when I kept searching, what is lacking in my understanding of a Divine Being if I am not finding peace inside of me, unless I am in a particular place or with particular people? The answer for me was to stop looking in any one place, or to any one human being. It all came back to me, and my divinity, or lack thereof; that is the greatest teaching Vonnie showed me. I simply hadn't accepted the "free gift" given to me.

Vonnie showed me that in order to honor Him, I needed to "follow Him", let go of the "old" ways, change my thinking, and always, "move forward". All of the great Teachers were about a Promise, the kind of promise that exists here and now, and for eternity. It is a promise of hope and joy and goodness and smiles and laughter and affection and love for today, tomorrow and forever. It is the promise of eternal life and the one that tells us we are a part of the Divine, if we choose to accept it, and leave behind any guilt or shame or hurt, and the "old" thinking that we are doomed to be a "sinner". Remember, "He" gave us the Promise of being "saved". All the great Teachers provided a Promise so we would never silence our soul again. Honor Him, or the Others, and accept it. Vonnie wanted me to embrace that Promise, and I do not want to disappoint her.

CHAPTER TWENTY-FOUR

MY LAST WILL AND TESTAMENT

There are no more trials left for me.

The three persons in my life who loved me unconditionally, and reached into my child's heart, are gone from my life here. There is no doubt in my mind I will see them again. I feel lonely here, but not alone. Vonnie said to me many times, "always here for you". I know that to be as true today as it was before March 23, 2021.

My sister showed me eternal life the day she left this earthly existence. She provided healing for me over and over. She saw something in me that I had failed to see when she was here, mostly because I gave too much attention to those that had not found their own divine essence. I was humbled that she allowed me to be one of only two persons to be present with her as she transitioned to a new life. I didn't realize, until the day after, that she had passed on what was to have been my birthday. I agonized over this, along with my grief, until someone said to me, "what an honor!".

The times I sat on the bench connecting with the stars and trying to awaken my soul again, I had another wonder filled delight. My sister knew how much I liked bunnies, so one night as I'm gazing at the stars, I looked down to see a bunny sitting beside me. I was thrilled and excited, the way a child would be. The bunny was to return on numerous nights. It moved me forward in my grief process.

"Believe in Miracles" was written on a piece of wood in my sister's home. I noticed it two weeks before she passed from this earth. All this and more led me back to where I needed to be, in that Connection with the One, and my soul essence. I silenced my soul again in 2010, and again in 2017, but Vonnie brought me "home", and I will see them both soon.

Ray was the third person to touch a little girl's heart. He was the strength that I needed in a father figure. He gave me encouragement and made me feel special. I will never forget all of the years of his caring. Thank you for being a man of integrity, courage and honor, and for making a child feel important. I love you always, and look forward to our time together again.

My final tribute is to my "best teacher", and my mother image....

Vonnie, You gave so much to so many. It is impossible to tell you of your value to me, and those that have known your heart and loved you. You gave me your wisdom and guidance, your kindness, your faith, your trust. You had a smile that would melt any child's heart. Your voice reverberated whenever you spoke, with a softness that was never frightening to a child, and served always to be reassuring. You knew the words to say to comfort a child. You had a heart like none other, a heart that children could feel and see and reach into. You loved all children unconditionally. Nothing is so sacred as that kind of love. You now know what I knew in my child's heart, and why I loved you as I did, and that has proved to be the greatest comfort to me.

And to my grandfather, who defined this life but also served as a memory that will never be forgotten in love and trust and family. I have felt your presence throughout my lifetime, and I know you will be the first to greet me on my journey home. Thank you. I love you forever.

This serves as my last will and testament ... I do hereby bequeath my childlike hope and joy and goodness and smiles and laughter and affection and love to anyone who will accept these, and pass them along to another earth being. I bequeath all my Love to children everywhere.

FINAL THOUGHTS...

May *your* soul awaken and find the Truth...

"Childlike love is irreplaceable, real and pure".

You don't have to be "saved"; you already are.

Doing it right means never having to express regrets.

The Divine light is in all of us; we only have to accept it.

Forgiveness is not a good thing; it is a God thing, and we are a part of the One; we are not the One.

Thoughts of our "best teacher" only bring hope and joy and goodness and laughter and smiles and affection.

It is not our place to forgive because it is not our place to judge.

It is important to make restitution for our mistakes because we are the only one responsible for our actions.

We were defined upon entering this earth. Find that definition inside you.

"Death" is an unending. It is part of everlasting life until it is no longer necessary.

The Great Teachers, like Jesus, didn't come to remind us that we are "sinners". They brought us the Light that is in all of us, if we accept it.

If we go through life believing we are a "sinner", then that is how we will view others. That leads to darkness for them and for us.

"He" is the Light that leads us on our path. Follow His example. No great Teacher wants to be "worshiped".

The answers only lie in your heart, in the stillness of the Light.

Anything that is not of Good is not of the Most Divine.

The answers do not lie in anyone or anything outside of you, but within the Greater you, the divine in you that exists from that place of Oneness.

Build a tree stand, and find that place of Oneness.

EPILOGUE...

A Prescription for My Life...

Most medical doctors agree on one thing. The vast majority of patients they see are diseased because of stress, and because of the lifestyles we choose to live. In actuality it would be difficult to find a disease that is not preventable. In listening to my awakened soul, I yielded the following prescription for my life; my hope is that you will develop a similar prescription and find the courage to follow it despite the beliefs of others.

Every morning upon waking I will engage in quiet meditation for one half hour.

Every morning after meditation I will nourish my body only enough to sustain it.

Every morning with or after my nourishment I will take the supplements that are healthful to the needs of my body.

Every morning I will drink 16 ounces of water.

Each morning of every day I will search for the child in me.

Each morning of every day for the rest of my life I will be kind to someone, especially a child.

Everyday I will engage in a physical activity that will remind me that my body is a temple.

Everyday I will nourish my body only for need, not pleasure.

Every afternoon I will drink 16 ounces of water.

Each afternoon of every day I will search for the child in me.

Each afternoon of every day for the rest of my life I will be kind to someone, especially a child.

Every evening I will express gratitude for all that I experienced in this day, and the one that follows.

Each evening of every day I will search for the child in me.

Each evening of every day for the rest of my life I will be kind to someone, especially a child.

Each night before falling off to sleep I will strengthen my soul with quiet so that I am prepared for whatever path I must follow with the dawn of the new day.

Each night I will remind myself that with each new dawn I must play, laugh, believe in wishes, and listen for my truth, and that of my Creator, so that I know I have prepared myself for everlasting life.

RECIPE FOR HAPPINESS

Ingredients:

1   *Child*
1   defined *self*
1   full cup *divine love*   Sun baked *Play*
1   whole *Present*   Many *kind gestures*
1   tender *Appreciation of Life*   1 defined *Creator*
1   *whole heart*
1   *chosen family*   *Times Alone*

Directions:

Warm the *Child* to room temperature.

Add to the *Child*, 1 *chosen family.*

Combine 1 defined *Creator* with 1 defined *self.* <u>Gently</u> stir together with the *Child* and *chosen family,* and place in a round "see through" cake pan.

In a separate bowl mix together 1 whole *Present* with 1 tender *Appreciation of Life,* many *kind gestures, Times Alone,* and 1 *whole heart.* Add this mixture to the "see through" cake pan ingredients.

Sprinkle on top this "see through" cake, the Sun baked *Play* and 1 full cup *divine love. Bake every day, at the temperature best suited for you, for the rest of your earthly existence.* Serve with your favorite fruit or ice cream. Eat generously, and share generously, your new "happiness"! Enjoy!

ACKNOWLEDGMENTS...

(I would be sadly remiss if I didn't acknowledge all of the aunts and uncles and cousins, and other grandparents who served as family to me in their support and love. I will always be grateful for their examples and encouragement along the way. And to my best friend, and her grandson, Max, and for countless friends, and "strangers", especially the man who was there in DC on February 7, 2004; thank you for being in my life when it mattered most. But particularly to my magically wonderful nieces and nephews, as you filled my heart with joy and laughter and love, and served as the impetus for my work and love for all children. I'm grateful to you all.)

PROCEEDS FROM THE SALE OF THIS BOOK WILL BE GIVEN TO ST. JUDE'S RESEARCH HOSPITAL...
...IN MEMORY OF DANIEL.

Daniel was diagnosed with osteosarcoma, and left this earth at the age of 19. He held a special place in his heart for the children at St. Jude's. He was a wonderful young man who loved his "Nan" dearly.

Made in the USA
Las Vegas, NV
16 January 2022

41483552R00069